A Grandparent's Devotional

Close to My Heart

40 Weeks of Scripture, Prayer and Reflection

for Your Grandchild

Rebekah Tague

Introduction

Your grandchild has a very special piece of your heart, and as a grandparent, your influence in their life is remarkably special. When you give the precious gift of time and love to your grandchild and prioritize them as an important part of your life, the impact can last for generations. There is no better way to show Christ's love than to actively pray for your grandchild. Whether they are a very young infant or a grown adult, the impact of your prayers can alter and change the direction of their life. God can use you, his faithful servant, to be a strong encourager and prayer warrior for your grandchild. Even if your grandchild is far from the Lord right now, prayer with faith is your best and greatest hope. Prayer also knows no distance. If you are far away from your grandchild, the fact that they know you are praying for and thinking about them is incredibly significant.

This book is a tangible way to let your grandchild know you are praying for them. The book contains 40 different prayer themes. Each day consists of a short verse and prayer that corresponds to the weekly theme. Throughout the book there are many opportunities for you to bless your grandchild by writing down personalized notes, thoughts and memories that they can read and reflect upon through their life. There are also places for you to include pictures of your choice that you would like your grandchild to keep. This book is a prayer legacy book. After you are through, give the book to your grandchild. By taking the time to pray daily for your grandchild you are leaving a strong Christian legacy and a godly inheritance. You are letting them know that you deeply love and care for them and that they are so very close to your heart. There is no greater gift.

Weekly Themes

PLACE
PICTURE OVER
FRAME

Week 1

Created by God

Create:

To beget, to generate, to bring forth

Day 1

The Spirit of God has made me, and the breath of the Almighty gives me life.

JOB 33:4

You have handcrafted my grandchild and breathed life into them. Because of you God, they live and function. Let them realize that every breath they take is a gift from you. You are the Amazing Creator! My grandchild is remarkable, your work of art. Help them to know their great value and worth because they have been created by you.

Day 2

The hearing ear and the seeing eye, the LORD has made both of them.

PROVERBS 20:12

You, the God of the Universe, have handcrafted my grandchild. You made their eyes and ears and all their body parts. You have given them a beating heart and a working brain. Your creation is something to behold. I give you praise!

Day 3

For since the creation of the world His invisible attributes, His eternal power and divine nature, have been clearly seen, being understood through what has been made, so that they are without excuse.

ROMANS 1:20

God, creation speaks of your presence and existence. When I look at my grandchild, I see your fingerprints all over them and gain new insight and understanding about you. Thank you that they are a testimony to who you are.

Day 4

For we are His workmanship, created in Christ Jesus for good works, which God prepared beforehand so that we would walk in them.

EPHESIANS 2:10

You created my grandchild for a purpose. You have already planned out tasks for them to do which will bless others. Help them to walk on your path and accomplish what you have set for them to complete.

Day 5

God created man in His own image, in the image of God He created him; male and female He created them.

GENESIS 1:27

Thank you for the beautiful differences between male and female. Let my grandchild grow to be a reflection of what you intended and please help them find their identity in you Jesus.

Day 6

Great are the works of the LORD; they are studied by all who delight in them.

PSALM 111:2

When I look into the eyes of my grandchild I want to praise you Lord! My grandchild is designed by you. Great are your works! Your hand has formed every aspect of them and I stand in wonder praising you!

Day 7

When I consider Your heavens, the work of Your fingers, the moon and the stars, which You have ordained; what is man that You take thought of him, and the son of man that You care for him? Yet You have made him a little lower than angels, and You crown him with glory and majesty!

PSALM 8:3-5

You the creator of the sky, the billions of stars, the moon and all of creation, have made my grandchild. I am so thankful that you care for them and that you take notice of every detail of their life. May they experience your crowning of glory and honor. Let them have a deep sense of value and belonging because you love them and because I love them.

God did an excellent job when he made you...

_____

_____

_____

_____

_____

_____

_____

I remember when you were born...

_____

_____

_____

_____

_____

_____

_____

_____

_____

_____

_____

_____

_____

Week 2

The Gift of Salvation

Salvation:

The redemption of man from the bondage of sin and liability to eternal death, and the conferring on him everlasting happiness

Day 1

…that if you confess with your mouth Jesus as Lord, and believe in your heart that God raised Him from the dead, you will be saved…

ROMANS 10:9

Please prepare the heart of my grandchild to accept and believe in you, your death and resurrection. Help them to seek your forgiveness and receive you into their life. Help them to believe fully all the truths in the Bible.

Day 2

"Come now, and let us reason together," says the LORD, "Though your sins are as scarlet, they will be as white as snow; though they are red like crimson, they will be like wool…"

ISAIAH 1:18

You are a forgiving God. Let my grandchild realize that they have a sin problem and that you are the only solution. Help them to humble their heart before you. Thank you for your grace. Help my grandchild to know how valuable they are and how much they are worth. You gave your life for them because of your love.

Day 3

The Lord is not slow about His promise, as some count slowness, but is patient toward you, not wishing for any to perish but for all to come to repentance.

2 PETER 3:9

Thank you for your patience with my grandchild. Please help me as a grandparent to be loving, kind and patient with them as well. I pray Lord, that they will be faithful and steadfast in walking with you throughout their lifetime.

Day 4

The LORD your God is in your midst, a victorious warrior. He will exult over you with joy, He will be quiet in His love, He will rejoice over you with shouts of joy.

ZEPHANIAH 3:17

You are a Mighty Warrior. You have rescued us from a life of sin and a dark eternity. Thank you for reconciling us back with you forever. Thank you that you will rejoice in, and sing over, my grandchild.

Day 5

God is faithful, through whom you were called into fellowship with His Son, Jesus Christ our Lord.

1 CORINTHIANS 1:9

As temptations arise and the pressures from this world to deny you increase, thank you for your faithful support for my grandchild. Give them strength to stand strong in their faith.

Day 6

Now the Lord is the Spirit, and where the Spirit of the Lord is, there is liberty. But we all, with unveiled face, beholding as in a mirror the glory of the Lord, are being transformed into the same image from glory to glory, just as from the Lord, the Spirit.

2 CORINTHIANS 3:17-18

Please help my grandchild's faith (or future faith) to be backed by godly actions and a Christ like transformation. Help them to experience freedom from the bondage of sin because they belong to you. You are in charge of the future.

Day 7

For I am confident of this very thing, that He who began a good work in you will perfect it until the day of Christ Jesus.

PHILIPPIANS 1:6

You are actively working in the life of my grandchild. From the moment of conception, you started your plan for them. Thank you that you will continue to draw them close to you throughout their life until they meet you in person.

Giving your life to Jesus is the absolute best decision because...

_____

_____

_____

_____

_____

_____

_____

_____

This is the story about how I became a Christian...

_____

_____

_____

_____

_____

_____

_____

_____

_____

_____

_____

_____

_____

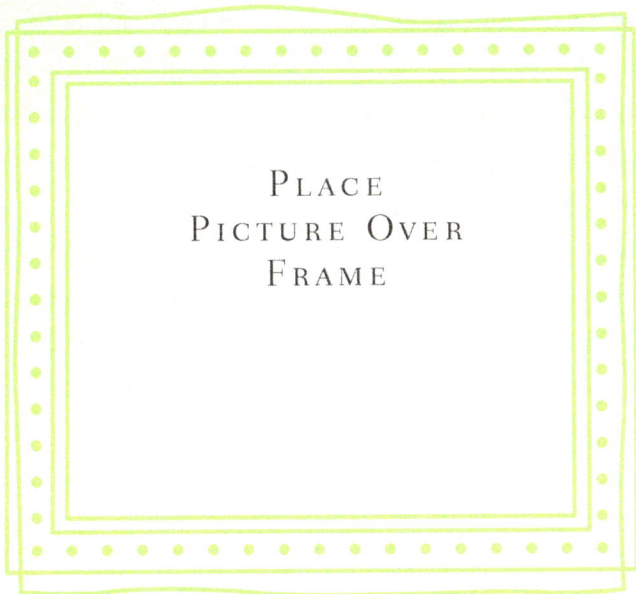

PLACE
PICTURE OVER
FRAME

PLACE
PICTURE OVER
FRAME

Week 3

Wellness in mind, body and soul

Well:

BEING IN HEALTH; HAVING A SOUND BODY,
WITH A REGULAR PERFORMANCE OF THE NATURAL
AND PROPER FUNCTIONS

Day 1

Beloved, I pray that in all respects you may prosper and be in good health, just as your soul prospers.

3 JOHN 1:2

In addition to good health, I pray that my beloved grandchild's soul will prosper. Though everyone is born with spiritual brokenness, thank you Lord that you restore. Help them to experience this restoration by accepting you as their Savior.

Day 2

Is anyone among you sick? Then he must call for the elders of the church and they are to pray over him, anointing him with oil in the name of the Lord...

JAMES 5:14

Thank you Father that we can come to you with the burden of sickness. If sickness comes to my grandchild, we can gather with others and pray for healing in your name. Thank you that you hear our prayers.

Day 3

You shall work six days, but on the seventh day you shall rest; even during plowing and harvest time you shall rest.

EXODUS 34:21

Life can be so busy and pull us in all different directions. I pray for my grandchild, that they will know the importance of rest and the balance between work, play and commitments. Help them to take time to relax.

Day 4

Many are the afflictions of the righteous, but the LORD delivers him out of them all. He [the Lord] keeps all his bones, not one of them is broken.

PSALM 34:20

This verse is referring to your promise to deliver those who are righteous. Please help my grandchild to honor you. Keep their bones from breaking and keep them free from major injury.

Day 5

But you shall serve the LORD your God, and He will bless your bread and your water; and I will remove sickness from your midst.

EXODUS 23:25

Lord, these were your words to the Israelites. You have the ability to take away sickness. Please keep your healing hand on my grandchild. When they get sick, please be merciful and bring healing to their life. Protect and spare them from illness as much as possible.

Day 6

A joyful heart is good medicine, but a broken spirit dries up the bones.

PROVERBS 17:22

When my grandchild has a difficult day help them to turn to you. Give them mental wellness and stability. Though hard times may come, help their spirit not to be crushed.

Day 7

Your eyes have seen my unformed substance; and in Your book were all written the days that were ordained for me, when as yet there was not one of them.

PSALM 139:16

Each day of life is already planned out for my grandchild. Please Lord, give their body strength, their mind soundness and stability, and their spirit and soul emotional health as they live out the days you have ordained.

I'm praying specifically for...

_____

_____

_____

_____

_____

_____

_____

_____

_____

_____

_____

Week 4

Christ Follower

Follower:

ONE THAT TAKES ANOTHER AS HIS GUIDE IN
DOCTRINES, OPINIONS OR EXAMPLE

Day 1

...for it is God who is at work in you, both to will and to work for His good pleasure. Do all things without grumbling or disputing; so that you will prove yourselves to be blameless and innocent, children of God above reproach in the midst of a crooked and perverse generation, among whom you appear as lights in the world, holding fast the word of life...

PHILIPPIANS 2:13-16

Father, you work in us to fulfill your good purpose. Please work in the heart of my grandchild. Help them to strive toward purity and righteous living. As they hold fast to you and your word, let the evidence of your presence shine brightly through them so that others can see.

Day 2

Suffer hardship with me, as a good soldier of Christ Jesus.

2 TIMOTHY 2:3

Jesus, sometimes following you is not easy and it may include suffering. Please give my grandchild the strength to follow you even though it may be tough. Show them how to be a strong and courageous soldier, let them not shrink back but move toward you. Walk closely with them in those hard times.

Day 3

But flee from these things, you man of God, and pursue righteousness, godliness, faith, love, perseverance and gentleness. Fight the good fight of faith; take hold of the eternal life to which you were called...

1 TIMOTHY 6:11-12

Give my grandchild the strength and endurance to fight for your truths and flee temptation. Let them pursue righteousness, godliness, faith, love and gentleness. Help them to hold fast to their confession of faith throughout their lifetime.

Day 4

Only conduct yourselves in a manner worthy of the gospel of Christ...
PHILIPPIANS 1:27

What a high calling. I pray this for my grandchild. Please guide them to act in a way that reflects a changed heart and life because of Christ. There will be situations where this is difficult but help them to follow you in those times.

Day 5

Therefore, we are ambassadors for Christ, as though God were making an appeal through us; we beg you on behalf of Christ, be reconciled to God.
2 CORINTHIANS 5:20

Help my grandchild be your ambassador and represent you well. Let them confess sin and be reconciled to you Lord. Help them to live in a way that will bring peace to their soul.

Day 6

For God so loved the world, that He gave His only begotten Son, that whoever believes in Him shall not perish, but have eternal life.
JOHN 3:16

Thank you for your love Father. Please help my grandchild to understand their sinful nature and their need for you. May they seek your forgiveness, believe in Jesus and take joy in the hope of eternal life.

Day 7

Finally, be strong in the Lord and in the strength of His might. Put on the full armor of God, so that you will be able to stand firm against the schemes of the devil.

EPHESIANS 6:10

There is another unseen realm that is actively fighting to distract my grandchild away from following you Lord. Please prepare them to be strong in Christ. Equip them with your "armor" and give them discernment so that they can fight off the devil's schemes. Help them to stand in your truth and follow you in this evil and scary world.

Following Jesus isn't always easy, but it's worth it...

_____

_____

_____

_____

_____

_____

_____

Here are some ways that I can see God at work in your life...

_____

_____

_____

_____

_____

_____

_____

_____

_____

_____

_____

_____

A Surrendered Life

Surrender:

TO YIELD TO THE POWER OF ANOTHER

Day 1

The plans of the heart belong to man, but the answer of the tongue is from the LORD. All the ways of a man are clean in his own sight, but the LORD weighs the motives.
Commit your works to the LORD and your plans will be established.

PROVERBS 16:1-3

Lord, please help my grandchild to commit their life to you. I pray that they will hand their plans over to you and that you will work in their life as you please. May Christ be glorified through their committed life.

Day 2

But prove yourselves doers of the word, and not merely hearers who delude themselves.

JAMES 1:22

Please help my grandchild to actively follow what you say Jesus. Please help them to surrender their life to you so that they will want to follow you as they hear what you are telling them.

Day 3

Submit therefore to God. Resist the devil and he will flee from you.

JAMES 4:7

Please help my grandchild to submit themselves to you God. Help them to actively resist the temptations of the devil with your help. I pray that you will keep the devil away from my grandchild. Protect them from evil as they surrender to you Father.

Day 4

Then Jesus said to His disciples, "If anyone wishes to come after Me, he must deny himself, and take up his cross and follow Me. For whoever wishes to save his life will lose it; but whoever loses his life for My sake will find it."

MATTHEW 16:24-25

Please help my grandchild, in every situation they may face, to choose you with all their heart. Help them to deny their sinful desires and follow you on a daily basis. Jesus give them the strength to walk with you throughout their life.

Day 5

He [God] said, "Do not stretch out your hand against the lad, and do nothing to him; for now I know that you fear God, since you have not withheld your son, your only son, from Me."

GENESIS 22:12

Abraham was willing to give up his only son Isaac in the most drastic way because you asked him to. Abraham withheld nothing from you Lord. I too, hand over my precious grandchild to you. Please be merciful to them.

Day 6

She [Hannah] made a vow and said, "O LORD of hosts, if You will indeed look on the affliction of Your maidservant and remember me, and not forget Your maidservant, but will give Your maidservant a son, then I will give him to the LORD all the days of his life…"

I SAMUEL 1:11

Lord, thank you so much for this gift of my grandchild. Just as Hannah in the Bible surrendered her son to you, I surrender the life of my grandchild to you. I plead with you Lord, that you will help them to follow you with their life.

Day 7

Peter began to say to Him, "Behold, we have left everything and followed You [Jesus]."

MARK 10:28

The disciples gave up everything to follow you Jesus. Help my grandchild to have this same attitude. Help them to be willing to surrender their life to follow you, no matter where you may direct.

Thoughts about letting God lead...

_____

_____

_____

_____

_____

_____

_____

_____

_____

_____

_____

PLACE
PICTURE OVER
FRAME

PLACE
PICTURE OVER
FRAME

Week 6

Christian Heritage and Identity

Heritage:

THE SAINTS OR PEOPLE OF GOD ARE CALLED HIS HERITAGE, AS BEING CLAIMED BY HIM, AND THE OBJECTS OF HIS SPECIAL CARE

Day 1

Therefore if anyone is in Christ, he is a new creature; the old things passed away; behold, new things have come.

2 CORINTHIANS 5:17

I praise you Lord because once we belong to you, we are a new creation! Please help my grandchild to experience the transformation of your presence in their life.

Day 2

He predestined us to adoption as sons through Jesus Christ to Himself, according to the kind intention of His will…

EPHESIANS 1:5

Thank you Jesus that we are adopted into your family. I am trusting you that my precious grandchild is predestined to experience your saving grace.

Day 3

…our old self was crucified with Him, in order that our body of sin might be done away with, so that we would no longer be slaves to sin…

ROMANS 6:6

As my grandchild takes on a new identity in Christ, help them to no longer be a slave to sin. Instead, let them be commanded by you Jesus. Let their life take on new meaning and purpose as you work within their heart.

Day 4

Before I formed you in the womb I knew you, and before you were born I consecrated you...

JEREMIAH 1:5

Lord, you have known my grandchild since before they were born. You have set them apart for your specific plans and purposes. There is a reason for their life. You have chosen their existence. Help them to follow you.

Day 5

But you are a chosen race, a royal priesthood, a holy nation, a people for God's own possession, so that you may proclaim the excellencies of Him who has called you out of darkness into His marvelous light...

1 PETER 2:9

My grandchild is yours Father. Help them to declare your excellence and goodness all their life. Call them out of darkness and let them experience the light of your presence.

Day 6

He created them male and female, and He blessed them and named them Man in the day when they were created.

GENESIS 5:2

You planned the identity of my grandchild before birth and since the beginning of time, you have shown your perfect will to mankind. Please help my grandchild to walk in, and embrace, the God-given identity you have created for them.

Day 7

...in reference to your former manner of life, you lay aside the old self, which is being corrupted in accordance with the lusts of deceit, and that you be renewed in the spirit of your mind, and put on the new self, which in the likeness of God has been created in righteousness and holiness of the truth.

EPHESIANS 4:22-24

As my grandchild goes through their life, help them to practice walking with you. Let them strive to put off their sinful nature and renew their mind in Christ on a daily basis.

God has a purpose for your life...

Week 7

A Deep Trust in God

Trust:

CONFIDENCE; A RELIANCE OR RESTING OF THE MIND ON THE
INTEGRITY, VERACITY, JUSTICE, FRIENDSHIP OR OTHER SOUND
PRINCIPLE OF ANOTHER PERSON

Day 1

Then he [Abram] believed in the LORD; and He [the Lord] reckoned it to him as righteousness.

GENESIS 15:6

Please Lord, like Abraham, may my grandchild believe what you say. Help their belief in your promises to grow as they walk with you.

Day 2

And those who know Your name will put their trust in You, for You, O LORD, have not forsaken those who seek You.

PSALM 9:10

I ask that my grandchild will know you as their best friend and learn that they can call out to you whenever they need help. As they trust in you, may they experience your faithfulness and understand that you will never leave them.

Day 3

Those who trust in the LORD are as Mount Zion, which cannot be moved but abides forever.

PSALM 125:1

When we trust in you Lord, we stand firm like a mountain. We have the joy of your presence with us in this life and the hope of eternal life in Heaven. Please help my grandchild to know the security that can be found in you.

Day 4

For the word of the LORD is upright, and all His work is done in faithfulness. He loves righteousness and justice; the earth is full of the lovingkindness of the LORD. By the word of the LORD the heavens were made, and by the breath of His mouth all their host.

PSALM 33:4-6

Father, your words are true. When you spoke, the heavens and billions of galaxies in the universe were formed. You give words of promise to us. May my grandchild know deep in their heart that they serve a great and mighty God who is trustworthy.

Day 5

And we know that God causes all things to work together for good to those who love God, to those who are called according to His purpose.

ROMANS 8:28

Father, thank you that you have called my grandchild to be your child. As they come to know you, let them take comfort in the fact that they can trust you. Help them to see that you will work out everything for good in their life.

Day 6

Now, O Lord GOD, You are God, and Your words are truth, and You have promised this good thing to Your servant.

2 SAMUEL 7:28

Please help my grandchild to know that you are holy and sovereign and that your word is trustworthy. Let them experience the good promises you have in store for those who trust in you.

Day 7

Now may the God of hope fill you with all joy and peace in believing, so that you will abound in hope by the power of the Holy Spirit.

ROMANS 15:13

Please give my grandchild joy and peace as they grow to trust you. As they are filled with your Spirit, bless them with a deep and overflowing hope that anchors them in your truth.

Let me tell you about a time when I had to really trust God...

Week 8

A Good Heart

Good:

Having moral qualities best adapted to its design and use, or the qualities which God's law requires; virtuous; pious; religious

Day 1

But the LORD said to Samuel, "Do not look at his appearance or at the height of his stature, because I have rejected him; for God sees not as man sees, for man looks at the outward appearance, but the LORD looks at the heart."

1 SAMUEL 16:7

Father, you are looking at what goes on inside our hearts and not at our appearances. I pray that you will help my grandchild to have a good heart. Foster qualities in them that will bring joy to you.

Day 2

Now Joseph, a Levite of Cyprian birth, who was also called Barnabas by the apostles (which translated means Son of Encouragement)…

ACTS 4:36

Just as Joseph's friends called him Barnabas because he was an encourager, help my grandchild to be known for having a heart of encouragement. Because of this, help other people to be blessed and strengthened in their own faith.

Day 3

The good man out of the good treasure of his heart brings forth what is good; and the evil man out of the evil treasure brings forth what is evil; for his mouth speaks from that which fills his heart.

LUKE 6:45

Please help my grandchild to be filled with your Spirit so that their heart is full of attributes like kindness, patience and joy. Let their words and actions show that their heart is good and pure. As a grandparent, help me to set a godly example as I do my part to model your love and kindness to them.

Day 4

Where you die, I will die, and there I will be buried. Thus may the LORD do to me, and worse, if anything but death parts you and me.

RUTH 1:17

Ruth had a good heart and was loyal to her mother-in-law and honored God. May my grandchild have a godly heart like Ruth. Let them be loyal to you Jesus and faithful to the people they grow to love and cherish.

Day 5

Here is a boy with five small barley loaves and two small fish, but how far will they go among so many?

JOHN 6:9

This boy was willing to share all that he had in his lunch. May my grandchild be kind and generous like this boy. Let them be willing to share. Please bless and multiply their generous acts and use their kindness to make a difference in the lives of others.

Day 6

Greet Prisca and Aquila, my fellow workers in Christ Jesus…

ROMANS 16:3

Priscilla and Aquila were Paul's co-workers in furthering the gospel. Please help my grandchild to have the desire and ability to work well with others so they can share about your kingdom. Instill in them a heart of reliability and camaraderie.

Day 7

Gaius, host to me and to the whole church, greets you...

ROMANS 16:23

Like Gaius, please help my grandchild to be hospitable by caring for others. Let them learn to grow in the gift of hospitality to make other people feel valued and welcomed in their presence.

You have some amazing qualities...

I'm really impressed with how you...

_____

_____

_____

_____

_____

_____

_____

_____

_____

_____

_____

Week 9

A Giver and Receiver of Mercy

Mercy:

THAT BENEVOLENCE, MILDNESS OR TENDERNESS OF HEART
WHICH DISPOSES A PERSON TO OVERLOOK INJURIES, OR TO
TREAT AN OFFENDER BETTER THAN HE DESERVES

Day 1

Blessed are the merciful, for they shall receive mercy.

MATTHEW 5:7

Please bless my grandchild with an attitude of mercy. Help them to be merciful to others. In return when they make mistakes, let others be merciful toward them. Thank you that my grandchild is a recipient of your mercy and forgiveness.

Day 2

Therefore I urge you, brethren, by the mercies of God, to present your bodies a living and holy sacrifice, acceptable to God, which is your spiritual service of worship.

ROMANS 12:1

It is only by your mercy God, that we can live in a way that is acceptable to you. Please have mercy on my grandchild. Help them to dwell under your hand of mercy and let them worship you with their life.

Day 3

Be merciful, just as your Father is merciful.

LUKE 6:36

Thank you that you are a merciful and compassionate Father. Please help my grandchild to return this mercy example in the way they relate to other people.

Day 4

… but He [Jesus] said to him, "Go home to your people and report to them what great things the Lord has done for you, and how He had mercy on you."

MARK 5:19

There are countless examples in the Bible that show how you Jesus, had mercy on people. Please have mercy on my grandchild. Please do great things in their heart and life.

Day 5

For He [God] says to Moses, "I WILL HAVE MERCY ON WHOM I HAVE MERCY, AND I WILL HAVE COMPASSION ON WHOM I HAVE COMPASSION." So then it does not depend on the man who wills or the man who runs, but on God who has mercy.

ROMANS 9:15-16

We are completely dependent on your mercy toward us God. It is not by our own merit but by your grace that we belong to you. You are a sovereign and good Father, please have compassion on my grandchild and their family.

Day 6

For indeed he was sick to the point of death, but God had mercy on him, and not on him only but also on me, so that I would not have sorrow upon sorrow.

PHILIPPIANS 2:27

In hard times, please have mercy on my grandchild. Keep them from disaster. Please have mercy so that I will not have sorrow upon sorrow.

Day 7

The Lord grant mercy to the house of Onesiphorus, for he often refreshed me and was not ashamed of my chains

2 TIMOTHY 1:16

Just as Paul prayed for an outpouring of the Lord's mercy on his friend's household, I ask that you pour your mercy on my grandchild and their home.

I have seen God's mercy toward you...

_____

_____

_____

_____

_____

_____

_____

_____

Week 10

Righteous Living

Righteousness:

**MORALLY RIGHT OR JUSTIFIABLE;
VIRTUOUS**

Day 1

…Noah was a righteous man, blameless in his time; Noah walked with God.
GENESIS 6:9

You considered Noah a righteous man as you looked upon the Earth and saw the wild and godless crowd. While everyone else was involved in sin, he walked faithfully with you. Please work in the life of my grandchild, let them be righteous. No matter what everyone else is doing, help them to obey you.

Day 2

Since all these things are to be destroyed in this way, what sort of people ought you to be in holy conduct and godliness?
2 PETER 3:11

Material things are not going to last in this world. Help my grandchild to learn to value what lasts forever, heavenly treasures. May they strive toward holy and godly living all their days.

Day 3

The memory of the righteous is blessed, but the name of the wicked will rot.
PROVERBS 10:7

I pray that when my grandchild's name is spoken, the thought of them will bring joy and gladness to others. Work in their life so that their godly behavior will be a blessing to other people.

Day 4

…yet, with respect to the promise of God, he [Abraham] did not waver in unbelief but grew strong in faith, giving glory to God, and being fully assured that what God had promised, He was able also to perform. Therefore it was also credited to him as righteousness. Now not for his sake only was it written that it was credited to him, but for our sake also, to whom it will be credited, as those who believe in Him who raised Jesus our Lord from the dead…

ROMANS 4:20-24

Though things looked bleak for Abraham regarding your promises Lord, he believed your word. Because of his faith, he was considered righteous. I pray that like Abraham, my grandchild will trust your promises. Let them believe in Jesus, his death, resurrection and ascension. Thank you in advance for the righteousness they will have through faith in you.

Day 5

…and He Himself bore our sins in His body on the cross, so that we might die to sin and live to righteousness; for by His wounds you were healed.

1 PETER 2:24

The only way we can be righteous before you Jesus is to accept what you did for us. Help my grandchild to be able to die to sin and live for righteousness because of your death on the cross.

Day 6

Josiah was eight years old when he became king, and he reigned thirty-one years in Jerusalem. He did right in the sight of the LORD, and walked in the ways of his father David and did not turn aside to the right or to the left.

2 CHRONICLES 34:1-2

Josiah was young but he made godly decisions and had convictions to follow you with his whole heart. Just like Josiah, please keep my grandchild close to you. Get them on your path and then please, let them not turn to the right or left, but stay on your path.

Day 7

He [Hezekiah] trusted in the LORD, the God of Israel; so that after him there was none like him among all the kings of Judah, nor among those who were before him. For he clung to the LORD; he did not depart from following Him, but kept His commandments, which the LORD had commanded Moses.

2 KINGS 18:5-7

Like Hezekiah, please give my grandchild a strong faith and a deep trust in you Lord. Let them cling to you and live within your will. Please be with them and grant success. Help them to honor you, stand firm in their convictions and resist negative peer pressure.

Some favorite memories with you include...

_____

_____

_____

_____

_____

_____

_____

_____

_____

_____

_____

_____

Love Beyond Measure

Love:

TO BE PLEASED WITH; TO REGARD WITH AFFECTION ON
ACCOUNT OF SOME QUALITIES WHICH EXCITE PLEASING
SENSATIONS OR DESIRE OR GRATIFICATION

Day 1

But you are to cling to the LORD your God, as you have done to this day.

JOSHUA 23:8

Please help my grandchild to hold fast to you with a committed love. Let them understand who you are and what you have done for them.

Day 2

Therefore be imitators of God, as beloved children; and walk in love, just as Christ also loved you and gave Himself up for us, an offering and a sacrifice to God as a fragrant aroma.

EPHESIANS 5:1-2

Please help my grandchild to know they are dearly loved and cared for by me. Let them know that as their heavenly Father, you love them even more. Lead them to walk in a loving way toward others because of this.

Day 3

May the Lord direct your hearts into the love of God and into the steadfastness of Christ.

2 THESSALONIANS 3:5

God, your love for us is unending and pure. Please show my grandchild the depth, security and persistence of your love. Direct their heart toward you.

Day 4

Delight yourself in the LORD; and He will give you the desires of your heart.

PSALM 37:4

Let my grandchild delight in you Lord. Help them to realize that all the good and wonderful gifts in life are from you because of your love.

Day 5

But his delight is in the law of the LORD, and in His law he meditates day and night.
PSALM 1:2

As my grandchild learns new things about you, please help them to love and value your word and commands.

Day 6

And He answered, "You shall love the Lord your God with all your heart, and with all your soul, and with all your strength, and with all your mind, and your neighbor as yourself.
LUKE 10:27

As my grandchild grows, help them to love you with all their heart, soul, mind and strength. Equipped with this, let them grow in their capacity to love others.

Day 7

After He had removed him [Saul], He raised up David to be their king, concerning whom He also testified and said, "I have found David the son of Jesse, a man after My heart, who will do all My will."
ACTS 13:22

David loved you deeply. You called him your friend and a man after your own heart. Please help my grandchild to also serve and love you like David. Protect them from making the same mistakes as David.

There are so many reasons why I love you…

PLACE
PICTURE OVER
FRAME

PLACE
PICTURE OVER
FRAME

Week 12

Christian Mentoring and Support

Mentor:

TO INSTRUCT; TO INFORM; TO COMMUNICATE TO ANOTHER THE KNOWLEDGE OF THAT WHICH HE WAS BEFORE IGNORANT

Support:

TO BEAR; TO SUSTAIN; TO UPHOLD SPIRITS; VALOR

Day 1

Train up a child in the way he should go, even when he is old he will not depart from it.

PROVERBS 22:6

Father, I ask that you will help me as a grandparent to love and mentor my grandchild as much as I can by showing and teaching them about having a strong foundation in you and a godly moral compass.

Day 2

Iron sharpens iron, so one man sharpens another.

PROVERBS 27:17

Friends change in different seasons but I pray that in each season of my grandchild's life, there will be people that will encourage them to be stronger in character and more like you Jesus.

Day 3

Be imitators of me, just as I also am of Christ.

1 CORINTHIANS 11:1

As my grandchild walks through life, please provide good Sunday school teachers, church leaders and godly family and friends to be Christ like examples. Please put it on the hearts of these people to take active roles in supporting my grandchild's Christian growth.

Day 4

I thank God, whom I serve with a clear conscience the way my forefathers did, as I constantly remember you in my prayers night and day, longing to see you, even as I recall your tears, so that I may be filled with joy.

2 TIMOTHY 1:3-4

There is so much power in prayer. Thank you for those that pray for my grandchild and their family. Please continue to bring people into my grandchild's life that will remember them often in prayer.

Day 5

For I am mindful of the sincere faith within you, which first dwelt in your grandmother Lois and your mother Eunice, and I am sure that it is in you as well.

2 TIMOTHY 1:5

Father, let me as a grandparent leave a strong Christian legacy. Let this be passed down to my grandchild and in turn impact my great grandchildren and generations to come.

Day 6

And even when I am old and gray, O God, do not forsake me, until I declare your strength to this generation, your power to all who are to come.

PSALM 71:18

God, please help me to declare your strength and power to my grandchild. Give me the strength I need to do the tasks that you have laid out for me in regards to loving and teaching my grandchild. Thank you that I have a purpose, a calling and a very important assignment from you!

Day 7

Therefore, I exhort the elders among you, as your fellow elder and witness of the sufferings of Christ, and a partaker also of the glory that is to be revealed, shepherd the flock of God among you, exercising oversight not under compulsion, but voluntarily, according to the will of God; and not for sordid gain, but with eagerness; nor yet as lording it over those allotted to your charge, but proving to be examples to the flock. And when the Chief Shepherd appears, you will receive the unfading crown of glory. You younger men, likewise, be subject to your elders...

1 PETER 5:1-5

As a grandparent, I am accountable to you God, the Chief Shepherd. What an honor that you chose me to help guide and shepherd my grandchild. I can only do this with your assistance, so please give me wisdom as I invest in my grandchild. May they be receptive to you and respectful toward their elders.

Qualities of a godly mentor...

_____

_____

_____

_____

_____

_____

When I was young, I wish I knew that...

_____

_____

_____

_____

_____

_____

_____

_____

_____

_____

_____

_____

_____

_____

PLACE
PICTURE OVER
FRAME

PLACE
PICTURE OVER
FRAME

Week 13

Good Friends

Friend:

ONE WHO IS ATTACHED TO ANOTHER BY AFFECTION; ONE WHO ENTERTAINS FOR ANOTHER SENTIMENTS OF ESTEEM, RESPECT AND AFFECTION WHICH LEAD HIM TO DESIRE HIS COMPANY AND TO SEEK TO PROMOTE HIS HAPPINESS AND PROSPERITY

Day 1

You shall not follow the masses in doing evil, nor shall you testify in a dispute so as to turn aside after a multitude in order to pervert justice…

EXODUS 23:2

As my grandchild forms friendships in different life stages, help them to seek you for wisdom above popularity. Help them to honor what the Bible says, even if it may be unpopular.

Day 2

Then I [God] will come down and speak with you [Moses] there, and I will take of the Spirit who is upon you, and will put Him upon them; and they shall bear the burden of the people with you, so that you will not bear it all alone.

NUMBERS 11:17

God, you know that we need others to help us with responsibilities and burdens. In this passage, Moses needed support. Just as you provided others to share in the responsibility of leadership with Moses, please bring great Christian friends and mentors into my grandchild's life to help them when stressful times come.

Day 3

He who walks with wise men will be wise, but the companion of fools will suffer harm.

PROVERBS 13:20

Lord, when it comes to friends and companions, help my grandchild to pick wise people that love you. Also, please bring strong Christian friends into their life that can teach and show them your truths.

Day 4

Do not be deceived: "Bad company corrupts good morals."
1 CORINTHIANS 15:33

Guide my grandchild through the process of finding good friends. Help them to be discerning. Please protect them from bad company. Please lead them to good quality friendships and guard them from dangerous relationships.

Day 5

Jonathan made David vow again because of his love for him, because he loved him as he loved his own life.
1 SAMUEL 20:17

As my grandchild forms friendships, please bring at least one great Christian friend into their life for each season. Help them to not experience lonely days or years but always have a good friend that brings fun and laughter.

Day 6

Two are better than one because they have a good return for their labor. For if either of them falls, the one will lift up his companion. But woe to the one who falls when there is not another to lift him up.
ECCLESIASTES 4:9-10

Please bring reliable and loyal friends into my grandchild's life that will be there to serve as sources of encouragement, companionship and strength.

Day 7

The righteous is a guide to his neighbor, but the way of the wicked leads them astray.
PROVERBS 12:26

Please bless my grandchild with godly and stable Christian friends that can guide them closer to you. Jesus, you are with them to help them in making the right choices. Please give them wisdom with relationship decisions.

Thoughts about how to choose a good friend...

_____

_____

_____

_____

_____

_____

_____

_____

_____

God's Protection

Protect:

TO COVER OR SHIELD FROM DANGER OR INJURY; TO DEFEND;
TO GUARD; TO PRESERVE IN SAFETY

Day 1

Keep me as the apple of your eye; hide me in the shadow of Your wings…
PSALM 17:8

Father, thank you for keeping a close eye on my grandchild. This world is crazy, please protect them and keep them safe. Let your presence be a defense and a place of refuge for them. Today I specifically ask that you keep them from physical harm, car accidents and other types of dangerous incidents that could arise in the future.

Day 2

The LORD is my rock and my fortress and my deliverer, my God, my rock, in whom I take refuge; my shield and the horn of my salvation, my stronghold. I call upon the LORD, who is worthy to be praised, and I am saved from my enemies.
PSALM 18:2-3

Thank you Father that you are a rock, fortress and deliverer. Please be my grandchild's salvation and stronghold. Help them to know they can call on you at any time for protection. Please keep them safe from evil people like child molesters, traffickers, abusers and kidnappers.

Day 3

The LORD is your keeper; the LORD is your shade on your right hand. The sun will not smite you by day, nor the moon by night. The LORD will protect you from all evil; He will keep your soul. The LORD will guard your going out and your coming in from this time forth and forever.
PSALM 121:5-8

Thank you that you promise to watch over my grandchild and that you will protect them from harm. Please guard their life and soul. Please keep them healthy.

Day 4

Be strong and courageous, do not be afraid or tremble at them, for the LORD your God is the one who goes with you. He will not fail you or forsake you.

DEUTERONOMY 31:6

Thank you that my grandchild does not have to be afraid because you are always by their side. Help them to put their trust in you. Please protect them in scary or dangerous situations.

Day 5

May the LORD answer you in the day of trouble! May the name of the God of Jacob set you securely on high! May He send you help from the sanctuary and support you from Zion!…We will sing for joy over your victory, and in the name of our God we will set up our banners. May the LORD fulfill all your petitions…

PSALM 20:1-2 & 5

Please be close to my grandchild when they are worried or scared. Provide them with help Lord. Thank you for being faithful and for hearing my prayers.

Day 6

Because he has loved Me, therefore I will deliver him; I will set him securely on high, because he has known My name. He will call upon Me, and I will answer him; I will be with him in trouble; I will rescue him and honor him. With a long life I will satisfy him and let him see My salvation.

PSALM 91:14-16

Thank you that you will answer my grandchild and deliver them from harm. I ask that they will acknowledge your name and that you will give them a long and wonderful life.

Day 7

But the Lord is faithful, and He will strengthen and protect you from the evil one.

2 THESSALONIANS 3:3

Satan, like a roaring lion, is seeking to destroy. Thank you God for your promise to protect my grandchild from the devil's lies and schemes. Thank you that you will give them strength, safety and discernment.

My specific prayers of protection for you...

_____

_____

_____

_____

_____

_____

_____

_____

_____

Sexual Purity

Pure:

Free from moral defilement, Free from anything improper; Free from vice or moral turpitude

Day 1

How can a young man keep his way pure? By keeping it according to Your word.

PSALM 119:9

Father, I ask that my grandchild stay on the path of purity and follow your word as they navigate through life. Help them to have the desire for purity and realize that your word is the key to honorable living.

Day 2

Turn away my eyes from looking at vanity, and revive me in Your ways.

PSALM 119:37

I am specifically praying that my grandchild will be careful with what they watch. The pornography on the Internet and inappropriate media are everywhere. Help them to make good choices as teens and adults. Please help me as a grandparent to set a good example and safeguard my home from these evil influences.

Day 3

Flee immorality. Every other sin that a man commits is outside the body, but the immoral man sins against his own body.

1 CORINTHIANS 6:18

Protect my grandchild as they encounter situations where there may be opportunities for sexual immorality. Help them to flee for their life, to run from these temptations. Help them to be determined to follow you and to avoid placing themselves in situations that would encourage sin.

Day 4

Create in me a clean heart, O God, and renew a steadfast spirit within me.
PSALM 51:10

There are times when my grandchild will make mistakes but please help them to seek you for a new and pure mind. Help them to experience and understand the depth and breath of your forgiveness and love. You can wipe all mistakes completely clean and give them a new start any time they ask for your help and mercy.

Day 5

Establish my footsteps in Your word, and do not let any iniquity have dominion over me.
PSALM 119:133

Guide my grandchild's steps. Please help them follow your word and let no sin rule over them, including sexual sin. If they get lost or fall into sin, please bring them back to you. Show them that they can come to you if they are struggling and also seek the help and support of trustworthy people.

Day 6

Do not sharply rebuke an older man, but rather appeal to him as a father, to the younger men as brothers, the older women as mothers, and the younger women as sisters, in all purity.
1 TIMOTHY 5:1-2

As my grandchild interacts with other people, help them to treat the opposite sex with respect and purity. Help their heart to be honorable before you.

Day 7

"I, even I, am the one who wipes out your transgressions for My own sake,
And I will not remember your sins..."

ISAIAH 43:25

Help my grandchild to learn and practice self-control and to conduct their body in a holy and honorable way. If there are mistakes made, let them know that you are a good and holy God. Thank you for your abundance of grace and that you desire to make our lives new and clean as we commit to walking in your ways.

Some thoughts on the incredible value of purity...

_____

_____

_____

_____

_____

_____

_____

_____

Living with Integrity

Integrity:

WHOLENESS; PURITY; GENUINE

Day 1

...then I put Hanani my brother, and Hananiah the commander of the fortress, in charge of Jerusalem, for he was a faithful man and feared God more than many.

NEHEMIAH 7:2

The Bible says that this trusted person feared the Lord more than most people. Their attitude was full of reverence and honor for God. Please help my grandchild to be a person of integrity and upright character as well.

Day 2

Likewise urge the young men to be sensible; in all things show yourself to be an example of good deeds, with purity in doctrine, dignified, sound in speech which is beyond reproach, so that the opponent will be put to shame, having nothing bad to say about us.

TITUS 2:6-8

When my grandchild speaks and interacts with others, help their words to be sound and true. May their reputation be of great quality so others have nothing bad to say about them.

Day 3

Better is the poor who walks in his integrity than he who is crooked though he be rich.

PROVERBS 28:6

When it comes to money and finances, please help my grandchild to be a person of integrity. Whether they are in charge of a little money or a lot, help them to not cheat other people.

Day 4

…for we have regard for what is honorable, not only in the sight of the Lord, but also in the sight of men.

2 CORINTHIANS 8:21

Please give my grandchild wisdom to do what is right before you. Help them to follow your ways in the social settings they face so that they can be viewed as a reliable person of honesty and integrity. Let them represent you well Jesus.

Day 5

Let your eyes look directly ahead and let your gaze be fixed straight in front of you.

PROVERBS 4:25

When temptations pull on either side of my grandchild, please help them to fix their gaze on you Jesus. May they not be swayed by the alluring but empty things this world has to offer. Instead, help them to be sound in truth and a person of sincerity.

Day 6

He who walks blamelessly will be delivered, but he who is crooked will fall all at once.

PROVERBS 28:18

Please keep my grandchild safe as they walk in righteousness. Help them to follow your principles, and be a person of integrity, so they will not get stuck in sin.

Day 7

The LORD said to Satan, "Have you considered My servant Job? For there is no one like him on the earth, a blameless and upright man fearing God and turning away from evil. And he still holds fast his integrity, although you incited Me against him to ruin him without cause."

JOB 2:3

I first pray that you will spare my grandchild from Satan's attacks in contrast to what Job had to endure. I also ask that my grandchild will be a person of integrity, just like Job. Even in difficult times, help them not to compromise their values.

Sometimes it's hard to do the right thing, but it's worth it...

A favorite Bible verse I would like to share...

PLACE
PICTURE OVER
FRAME

PLACE
PICTURE OVER
FRAME

Week 17

God's Grace and Forgiveness

Grace:

THE FREE UNMERITED LOVE AND FAVOR OF GOD, THE SPRING
AND SOURCE OF ALL THE BENEFITS MEN RECEIVE FROM HIM

Day 1

For by grace you have been saved through faith; and that not of yourselves, it is the gift of God; not as a result of works, so that no one may boast.

EPHESIANS 2:8-9

Thank you for your mercy and grace upon my grandchild. Thank you for the gift of salvation and please help them to embrace it. Help them to begin to understand that your grace is incredibly deep.

Day 2

But if it is by grace, it is no longer on the basis of works, otherwise grace is no longer grace.

ROMANS 11:6

Help my grandchild to realize that salvation is due to your grace and that your love and approval do not have to be earned. Help their good works to come from a heart of gratitude toward you and not because they are desperate to win your favor.

Day 3

We love, because He first loved us.

1 JOHN 4:19

Any of the good and honorable qualities in us come from you. The love in our hearts is due to your grace because you decided to love us first. Help my grandchild to understand this.

Day 4

But when God, who had set me apart even from my mother's womb and called me through His grace, was pleased...

GALATIANS 1:15

Thank you that you have plans for my grandchild since their conception. Thank you that presently, they are being called by you as a recipient of your grace and mercy.

Day 5

What shall we say then? Are we to continue in sin so that grace may increase? May it never be! How shall we who died to sin still live in it?

ROMANS 6:1-2

As my grandchild experiences your grace, help them to realize that it is a precious gift. Let them not use it to their advantage but instead desire a closer walk with you. Help them not to play with sin but to stay well away from it.

Day 6

Grace and peace be multiplied to you in the knowledge of God and of Jesus our Lord...

2 PETER 1:2

Please Lord, let my grandchild experience the abundance of grace and peace that comes from knowing you. Let them know that when they make mistakes, your arms are open wide with forgiveness and mercy.

Day 7

He straightened up, and said to them, "He who is without sin among you, let him be the first to throw a stone at her." Again He stooped down and wrote on the ground. When they heard it, they began to go out one by one, beginning with the older ones, and He was left alone, and the woman, where she was, in the center of the court. Straightening up, Jesus said to her, "Woman, where are they? Did no one condemn you?" She said, "No one, Lord." And Jesus said, "I do not condemn you, either. Go. From now on sin no more.

JOHN 8: 7-11

Jesus, this woman in the Bible experienced your forgiveness and grace. Thank you that you have the same compassion for us. You redeem us and then ask us to change and sin no more. You forgive my grandchild when they make mistakes because no one is perfect. Help me to treat them as you would with kindness and compassion while at the same time encouraging them toward you Father.

I have seen God's grace poured upon your life in many ways...

_____

_____

_____

_____

_____

Contentment with Jesus

Content:

HELD; CONTAINED WITHIN LIMITS; HENCE, QUIET; NOT DISTURBED; HAVING A MIND AT PEACE; SATISFIED, SO AS NOT TO REPINE, OBJECT, OR OPPOSE

Day 1

Not that I speak from want, for I have learned to be content in whatever circumstances I am.
PHILIPPIANS 4:11

Help my grandchild to learn that an abundance of possessions does not bring happiness. Teach them that a solid relationship with you is what brings lasting contentment.

Day 2

I know how to get along with humble means, and I also know how to live in prosperity; in any and every circumstance I have learned the secret of being filled and going hungry, both of having abundance and suffering need. I can do all things through Him who strengthens me.
PHILIPPIANS 4:12-13

Lord, help my grandchild to be grateful with what they have. Give them the strength they need to be content in life no matter what situations they may face.

Day 3

Better is the little of the righteous than the abundance of many wicked.
PSALM 37:16

Above material wealth, I pray that my grandchild will be righteous before you and that they will have a strong relationship with you. This is more valuable than any abundance of possessions.

Day 4

Make sure that your character is free from the love of money, being content with what you have; for He Himself has said, "I will never desert you, nor will I ever forsake you"...

HEBREWS 13:5

Your presence Lord is the best gift. It is more valuable than money or anything else this world offers. Help my grandchild to keep a heavenly perspective when it comes to finances. Your help is priceless.

Day 5

But godliness actually is a means of great gain when accompanied by contentment. For we have brought nothing into the world, so we cannot take anything out of it either.

1 TIMOTHY 6:6-7

As a grandparent, help me to have an attitude of contentment. There is nothing we can take out of this world. Help my grandchild to see the benefit of being satisfied with what you have provided.

Day 6

Then He said to them, "Beware, and be on your guard against every form of greed; for not even when one has an abundance does his life consist of his possessions."

LUKE 12:15

Help my grandchild to take warning from Jesus and focus their priorities on what is lasting. Help them to discern a greedy attitude and guard against it.

Day 7

One hand full of rest is better than two fists full of labor and striving after wind.
ECCLESIASTES 4:6

When my grandchild works, help them to prioritize what is important. Instead of getting caught up in toiling for more stuff or higher status, let them experience contentment by enjoying life and spending time with the people they love.

Some things I've learned about contentment...

_____

_____

_____

_____

_____

_____

_____

_____

Here are some fun activities to do that are free...

_____

_____

_____

_____

_____

_____

_____

_____

_____

_____

_____

_____

A Wonderful Future Spouse

Future:

TIME TO COME; A TIME SUBSEQUENT TO THE PRESENT

Day 1

So she departed and went and gleaned in the field after the reapers; and she happened to come to the portion of the field belonging to Boaz, who was of the family of Elimelech.

RUTH 2:3

Lord, please do a similar work in my grandchild's life. Orchestrate circumstances so they can meet a wonderful spouse in your plan and time. Please provide someone good just like you did for Ruth and Boaz.

Day 2

Then the LORD God said, "It is not good for the man to be alone; I will make him a helper suitable for him."

GENESIS 2:18

I pray for my grandchild's spouse, asking that you will work in their heart at an early age. Help them to learn to love you so that they can love my grandchild in a Christ honoring way. Bless their future spouse's family.

Day 3

He said, "O LORD, the God of my master Abraham, please grant me success today, and show lovingkindness to my master Abraham. Behold, I am standing by the spring, and the daughters of the men of the city are coming out to draw water; now may it be that the girl to whom I say, 'Please let down your jar so that I may drink,' and who answers, 'Drink, and I will water your camels also'—may she be the one whom You have appointed for Your servant Isaac; and by this I will know that You have shown lovingkindness to my master."

GENESIS 24:12-19

Abraham's servant prayed a prayer of faith and you preformed a miracle. I pray you will help my grandchild not to compromise. Let them be successful in finding a quality spouse. Bring about someone who is considerate with good character.

Day 4

"For I know the plans that I have for you," declares the LORD, "plans for welfare and not for calamity to give you a future and a hope. Then you will call upon Me and come and pray to Me, and I will listen to you. You will seek Me and find Me when you search for Me with all your heart."

JEREMIAH 29:11-13

Lord, you have good plans for my grandchild, plans which may include a spouse. I pray both my grandchild and their spouse will each have a solid relationship with you. Thank you that you will hear their prayers and that you have a good plan for both of them.

Day 5

But seek first His kingdom and His righteousness, and all these things will be added to you.

MATTHEW 6:33

Please help my grandchild and their potential future spouse to serve others and be involved in ministries on their own before they meet. Help them to find purpose and meaning in life with Jesus as individuals.

Day 6

Do not be bound together with unbelievers, for what partnership have righteousness and lawlessness; or what fellowship has light with darkness?

1 CORINTHIANS 6:14

Give my grandchild the wisdom to marry a believer. Help them to be determined to seek out a spouse who loves you Jesus. Keep them from compromising.

Day 7

Two are better than one because they have a good return for their labor. For if either of them falls, the one will lift up his companion. But woe to the one who falls when there is not another to lift him up. Furthermore, if two lie down together they keep warm, but how can one be warm alone? And if one can overpower him who is alone, two can resist him. A cord of three strands is not quickly torn apart.

ECCLESIASTES 4:9-12

Bring my grandchild a supportive spouse and companion. Help them as a couple to enjoy each other's company, hold one another up in prayer and look out for each other with consideration. Help them to be tied to you Lord so that their marriage will be strong and thriving.

A prayer for your future...

_____

_____

_____

_____

_____

_____

_____

Good qualities to look for in a potential spouse...

_____

_____

_____

_____

_____

_____

_____

_____

_____

_____

_____

How I met my spouse...

_____

_____

_____

_____

_____

_____

_____

_____

_____

_____

_____

_____

_____

_____

PLACE
PICTURE OVER
FRAME

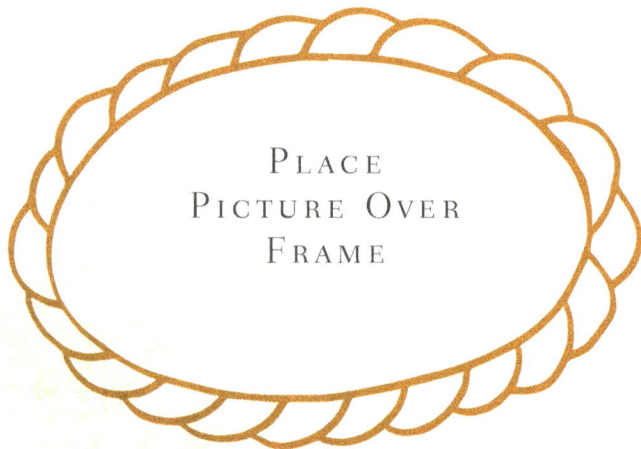

PLACE
PICTURE OVER
FRAME

Week 20

A Courageous Spirit

Courage:

BRAVERY; INTREPIDITY: THAT QUALITY OF MIND WHICH
ENABLES MEN TO ENCOUNTER DANGER AND DIFFICULTIES
WITH FIRMNESS, OR WITHOUT FEAR OR DEPRESSION OF
SPIRITS; VALOR

Day 1

Take care and be calm, have no fear and do not be fainthearted…

ISAIAH 7:4

There will be situations where my grandchild will be scared. In these times, help them to be careful and not rash, to be calm and not overcome with fear. Let them not lose heart, but know that you are with them.

Day 2

Have I not commanded you? Be strong and courageous! Do not tremble or be dismayed, for the LORD your God is with you wherever you go.

JOSHUA 1:9

Thank you that you promise to be with my grandchild. When discouragement creeps in, please give them strength and courage because they have you, the King of Heaven and Earth by their side.

Day 3

Now when Daniel knew that the document was signed, he entered his house (now in his roof chamber he had windows open toward Jerusalem); and he continued kneeling on his knees three times a day, praying and giving thanks before his God, as he had been doing previously.

DANIEL 6:10

When peer pressure tries to keep my grandchild from following you, help them to have courage like Daniel. He did not give up praying, even though it was against the law. Let them recognize that following you is more important than anything else.

Day 4

And when they had prayed, the place where they had gathered together was shaken, and they were all filled with the Holy Spirit and began to speak the word of God with boldness.
ACTS 4:31

Help my grandchild to have the courage to speak your name and tell others about you. Fill them with your Spirit so that they can be bold about their beliefs.

Day 5

Therefore let us draw near with confidence to the throne of grace, so that we may receive mercy and find grace to help in time of need.
HEBREWS 4:16

Please give my grandchild the courage to approach you without fear or hesitancy. Thank you for drawing my grandchild near to you. Remind them that in Christ they can be courageous, confident, fearless and secure. Help them to be able to share their needs and problems with you God.

Day 6

He Himself has said, "I will never desert you, nor will I ever forsake you," so that we confidently say, "The Lord is my helper, I will not be afraid. What will man do to me?"
HEBREWS 13:6

As my grandchild encounters a variety of situations, help them to have courage. You, the God of all creation, are holding their hand and you are their helper.

Day 7

The wicked flee when no one is pursuing, but the righteous are bold as a lion.

PROVERBS 28:1

As my grandchild grows to know you more, help them to have a clear conscience before you because of their righteousness in Christ. In this way, may they experience boldness and courage because they have nothing to hide.

Praying that God will give you courage in these specific areas...

_____

_____

_____

_____

_____

_____

_____

_____

Week 21

God's Faithful Presence

Presence:

THE EXISTENCE OF A PERSON OR THING IN A CERTAIN PLACE;
OPPOSED TO ABSENCE

Day 1

But the Lord stood with me and strengthened me, so that through me the proclamation might be fully accomplished, and that all the Gentiles might hear; and I was rescued out of the lion's mouth.

2 TIMOTHY 4:17

Thank you that your presence is very near to my grandchild. Help them know you are by their side. Fill them with your Spirit. Give them the strength to share their faith with others and to do what is right.

Day 2

I will ask the Father, and He will give you another Helper, that He may be with you forever…

JOHN 14:16

Your Holy Spirit will be with my grandchild to protect and advocate for them. Thank you for this promise. Help them to understand and learn more about the Holy Spirit's power.

Day 3

Where can I go from Your Spirit? Or where can I flee from Your presence? If I ascend to Heaven, You are there; if I make my bed in Sheol, behold, You are there. If I take the wings of the dawn, if I dwell in the remotest part of the sea, even there Your hand will lead me, and Your right hand will lay hold of me.

PSALM 139:7-10

No matter what we do or where we go, we can never be far from your presence. You will always guide us and hold our hand. As my grandchild goes through life may they know you will always be near. I entrust this much loved person to you Lord, knowing that you will take care of them.

Day 4

And He [the Lord] said, "My presence shall go with you, and I will give you rest."
EXODUS 33:14

Please surround my grandchild with your presence. In times when they feel afraid, comfort them with your peace and give them rest. Help them to be at peace because you are near.

Day 5

You will make known to me the path of life; in Your presence is fullness of joy; in Your right hand there are pleasures forever.
PSALM 16:11

Lord, thank you that no matter what happens on Earth, we will all be reunited with you in Heaven and filled with joy in your faithful presence. May my grandchild come to accept you as their Savior and experience joy with you in eternity.

Day 6

Do not fear, for I am with you; do not anxiously look about you, for I am your God. I will strengthen you, surely I will help you, surely I will uphold you with My righteous right hand.
ISAIAH 41:10

When scary or discouraging situations arise, please strengthen my grandchild. Help them to know that your presence will sustain, support and uphold them.

Day 7

Even though I walk through the valley of the shadow of death, I fear no evil, for You are with me; Your rod and Your staff, they comfort me.

PSALM 23:4

I pray for mercy on my grandchild when it comes to dark valleys and difficult days. I ask that if these situations arise, your presence will be like a brilliant sun giving them hope and comfort.

Thoughts about God's presence...

_____

_____

_____

_____

_____

_____

_____

_____

_____

Wisdom Beyond Measure

Wisdom:

THE RIGHT USE OR EXERCISE OF KNOWLEDGE; THE CHOICE OF LAUDABLE ENDS, AND OF THE BEST MEANS TO ACCOMPLISH THEM

Day 1

My son, if you will receive my words and treasure my commandments within you, make your ear attentive to wisdom, incline your heart to understanding; for if you cry for discernment, lift your voice for understanding; if you seek her as silver and search for her as for hidden treasures; then you will discern the fear of the LORD and discover the knowledge of God.

PROVERBS 2:1-5

I ask that my grandchild finds wisdom through reading the Bible. I pray that they will ask you for guidance and seek your truths. Help them to be receptive to your words.

Day 2

Discretion will guard you, understanding will watch over you…

PROVERBS 2:11

Help my grandchild to discern right from wrong. Give them the wisdom to make discerning choices and help them to see through facades that could lead them away from you Jesus. Let this discretion protect them from potentially dangerous situations.

Day 3

Listen to counsel and accept discipline, that you may be wise the rest of your days.

PROVERBS 19:20

Lord, please help my grandchild to be open to godly advice and counsel. Help them to be receptive to input and guidance. Help me to be able to lead them toward wisdom, and please let them listen.

Day 4

The Spirit of the LORD will rest on Him, the spirit of wisdom and understanding, the spirit of counsel and strength, the spirit of knowledge and the fear of the LORD. And He will delight in the fear of the LORD, and He will not judge by what His eyes see, nor make a decision by what His ears hear…

ISAIAH 11:2-3

This verse is describing Jesus. I also ask for these attributes to be displayed in my grandchild. Let your Spirit guide and direct them. Give them a delight for wisdom and understanding as well as a deep respect for you Father.

Day 5

Set up for yourself roadmarks, place for yourself guideposts; direct your mind to the highway, the way by which you went…

JEREMIAH 31:21

Please help my grandchild to take note of the path they take. Let them make wise decisions and not go down the roads that lead to destruction.

Day 6

Therefore be careful how you walk, not as unwise men but as wise, making the most of your time, because the days are evil. So then do not be foolish, but understand what the will of the Lord is. And do not get drunk with wine, for that is dissipation, but be filled with the Spirit…

EPHESIANS 5:15-18

Please God, help my grandchild to live wisely and not to waste time on activities that will steal their life and discernment. Keep them from the partying crowd. Help them not to abuse alcohol and to avoid drugs. Give them strength to stand up to peer pressure and not be led astray. Instead, may they be filled with your Spirit and pursue godliness.

Day 7

For the report of your obedience has reached to all; therefore I am rejoicing over you, but I want you to be wise in what is good and innocent in what is evil.

ROMANS 16:19

Lord, help my grandchild to be obedient to your principles with a heart of innocence. Let them avoid poor life choices. May they desire godliness and not be overtaken by evil influences.

I am praying that God will give you wisdom...

Some life lessons I would like to share with you...

The Ability to Discern

Discernment:

THE POWER OR FACULTY OF THE MIND, BY WHICH IT
DISTINGUISHES ONE THING FROM ANOTHER, AS TRUTH FROM
FALSEHOOD, VIRTUE FROM VICE

Day 1

And do not be conformed to this world, but be transformed by the renewing of your mind, so that you may prove what the will of God is, that which is good and acceptable and perfect.

ROMANS 12:2

Instead of conforming to peer pressure, help my grandchild to be transformed into who you want them to be. As they are transformed, let them clearly discern your will and direction for their life.

Day 2

Do not judge according to appearance, but judge with righteous judgment.

JOHN 7:24

It is so easy to judge by appearances. Help my grandchild to look deeper into the heart and motives of other people with discerning judgment.

Day 3

Woe to those who call evil good, and good evil; who substitute darkness for light and light for darkness; who substitute bitter for sweet and sweet for bitter! Woe to those who are wise in their own eyes and clever in their own sight! Woe to those who are heroes in drinking wine and valiant men in mixing strong drink...

ISAIAH 5:20-22

There are so many deceptive people who make evil seem acceptable. Please give my grandchild the ability to see through these schemes. Help them to be close enough to you and your word so that they understand what is good versus evil.

Day 4

For such men are false apostles, deceitful workers, disguising themselves as apostles of Christ. No wonder, for even Satan disguises himself as an angel of light. Therefore it is not surprising if his servants also disguise themselves as servants of righteousness, whose end will be according to their deeds.

2 CORINTHIANS 11:13-15

Give my grandchild discernment, especially when it comes to leaders in the church and selecting Christian friends. Help them to plainly see right from wrong even when there are many deceptive people in leadership positions.

Day 5

I am amazed that you are so quickly deserting Him who called you by the grace of Christ, for a different gospel; which is really not another; only there are some who are disturbing you and want to distort the gospel of Christ. But even if we, or an angel from heaven, should preach to you a gospel contrary to what we have preached to you, he is to be accursed!

GALATIANS 1:6-8

There are many teachings and philosophies that sound good, but are not according to your word. Help my grandchild to be able to discern this and not fall prey to deceptive teachings. Let your Spirit guide them.

Day 6

The LORD then spoke to Aaron, saying, "Do not drink wine or strong drink, neither you nor your sons with you, when you come into the tent of meeting... and so as to make a distinction between the holy and the profane, and between the unclean and the clean..."

LEVITICUS 10:8-10

Please help my grandchild not to partake or involve themselves in any activity which would cause them to lose their mental clarity and their ability to discern.

Day 7

Teach me good discernment and knowledge, for I believe in Your commandments.
PSALM 119:66

God, you are the ultimate teacher and your truths allow us to have sound judgment in life. Help my grandchild to trust your commands.

Here is an example of a time when God helped me to discern...

Godly Character

Character:

DISTINGUISHED OR GOOD QUALITIES; THOSE WHICH ARE
ESTEEMED AND RESPECTED

Day 1

Now, my daughter, do not fear. I will do for you whatever you ask, for all my people in the city know that you are a woman of excellence.

RUTH 3:11

I pray that my grandchild will grow up to be a man or woman of noble character, whose reputation is known to be honorable and excellent.

Day 2

And not only this, but we also exult in our tribulations, knowing that tribulation brings about perseverance; and perseverance, proven character; and proven character, hope; and hope does not disappoint, because the love of God has been poured out within our hearts through the Holy Spirit who was given to us.

ROMANS 5:3-5

Though I pray my grandchild will never have to go through difficult circumstances, you Lord do not promise this. However in such times instead of rejecting you, help my grandchild to follow you with perseverance. Let their character grow and their hope and trust in you remain strong.

Day 3

Finally, brethren, whatever is true, whatever is honorable, whatever is right, whatever is pure, whatever is lovely, whatever is of good repute, if there is any excellence and if anything worthy of praise, dwell on these things.

Philippians 4:8

Please help my grandchild to think and dwell upon true, right, noble, pure and admirable thoughts. Help their heart to overflow with a love for you and let it be evident in their character.

Day 4

Seek good and not evil, that you may live; and thus may the Lord God of hosts be with you, just as you have said!

AMOS 5:14

A person of good character is looking for good and not evil. I ask that my grandchild will be a seeker of pure and honorable things and not actively search for and take part in sinful activities.

Day 5

Let no unwholesome word proceed from your mouth, but only such a word as is good for edification according to the need of the moment, so that it will give grace to those who hear.

EPHESIANS 4:29

Help my grandchild to honor you with what comes from their mouth. When they speak to others, let their words bring life.

Day 6

My covenant with him [Levi] was one of life and peace, and I gave them to him as an object of reverence; so he revered Me and stood in awe of My name. True instruction was in his mouth and unrighteousness was not found on his lips; he walked with Me in peace and uprightness, and he turned many back from iniquity.

MALACHI 2:5-6

Lord help my grandchild to be filled with your Spirit, evident by noble character. Help them to speak the truth, have peace with you and motivate others to follow Jesus. Let them have a heart of reverence for your ways and respect your holy name.

Day 7

But now you also, put them all aside: anger, wrath, malice, slander and
abusive speech from your mouth.

COLOSSIANS 3:8

When my grandchild is with unbelievers, help them to stand out because of their
dedication to Jesus. May their words and actions be a testimony to their faith.

I've seen you display good character
traits...

_____

_____

_____

_____

_____

_____

_____

_____

A Legacy of Success

Success:

THE FAVORABLE OR PROSPEROUS TERMINATION OF ANYTHING ATTEMPTED; A TERMINATION WHICH ANSWERS THE PURPOSE INTENDED

Day 1

But just as you abound in everything, in faith and utterance and knowledge and in all earnestness and in the love we inspired in you, see that you abound in this gracious work also.

2 CORINTHIANS 8:7

In this verse, giving is described as a gracious work. Please help my grandchild to be successful in their understanding of the Bible and the practice of their faith. Help them to excel in their giving and generosity as their love for Jesus deepens.

Day 2

David was prospering in all his ways for the LORD was with him.

1 SAMUEL 18:14

We are only successful if you are with us Lord. Help my grandchild follow you, and in turn, bless them with success. Help them to know that great and small accomplishments come because of your presence and intervention.

Day 3

The LORD was with Joseph, so he became a successful man. And he was in the house of his master, the Egyptian. Now his master saw that the LORD was with him and how the LORD caused all that he did to prosper in his hand. So Joseph found favor in his sight and became his personal servant; and he made him overseer over his house, and all that he owned he put in his charge.

GENESIS 39:2-4

Like Joseph, I pray that your hand of favor will be on my grandchild. Please bring them success in their efforts. Bless and multiply the results of their attempts at various endeavors, let them be prosperous. Please give them favor in the eyes of their peers and superiors.

Day 4

Therefore everyone who hears these words of Mine and acts on them, may be compared to a wise man who built his house on the rock.

MATTHEW 7:24

Please help my grandchild to have clear and intelligent thinking. Help them to be successful with applying your words to their life.

Day 5

Sow your seed in the morning and do not be idle in the evening, for you do not know whether morning or evening sowing will succeed, or whether both of them alike will be good.

ECCLESIASTES 11:6

Please help my grandchild to understand the importance of working hard and the accomplishments that it brings. Please bless their efforts, keep them from idleness and help them to be prosperous.

Day 6

Without consultation, plans are frustrated, but with many counselors they succeed.

PROVERBS 15:22

Please help my grandchild to be open to the advice of those who are wise. Help them to seek the knowledge of God honoring people and be blessed by the counsel given. I ask that you Lord will be their ultimate counselor. Let them seek your advice frequently.

Day 7

For the LORD gives wisdom; from His mouth come knowledge and understanding. He stores up sound wisdom for the upright; He is a shield to those who walk in integrity...

PROVERBS 2:6-7

True success and the wisdom that comes with it is a gift from you Lord. Your definition of success is often different than what other people might perceive as successful. Help my grandchild to understand this heavenly version of success and live a life that is honorable according to your standards.

I am so proud of you because...

_____

_____

_____

_____

_____

_____

_____

_____

Talents and Abilities

Talent:

NATURAL GIFT OR ENDOWMENT

Day 1

As each one has received a special gift, employ it in serving one another as good stewards of the manifold grace of God.

1 PETER 4:10

Father, I pray that my grandchild will use the special abilities that you have given them to glorify you and to serve others. Let them be a good steward of what you have gifted.

Day 2

And there are varieties of ministries, and the same Lord. There are varieties of effects, but the same God who works all things in all persons.

1 CORINTHIANS 12:5-6

Please help my grandchild to find their niche in ministry. Lead them to utilize their gifts in the right place with the right people. Help other mentors to walk along side and encourage them in their abilities. Help my grandchild to be appreciative toward the talents that other people have instead of being envious.

Day 3

He also has put in his heart to teach, both he and Oholiab, the son of Ahisamach, of the tribe of Dan. He has filled them with skill to perform every work of an engraver and of a designer and of an embroiderer, in blue and in purple and in scarlet material, and in fine linen, and of a weaver, as performers of every work and makers of designs.

EXODUS 35:34-35

Thank you that you give these gifts. Just like you gave these people the ability to teach and do skilled work, please fill my grandchild with good gifts of ability that you see fit for them. Put it on their hearts to serve with the talents they have.

Day 4

And He [Christ] gave some as apostles, and some as prophets, and some as evangelists, and some as pastors and teachers, for the equipping of the saints for the work of service, to the building up of the body of Christ…
EPHESIANS 4:11-12

I ask that you will develop the spiritual gifts you have entrusted to my grandchild. Help me as a grandparent to notice and nurture these gifts. Let many in your church be blessed by my grandchild and their spiritual gifts.

Day 5

His master said to him, "Well done, good and faithful slave. You were faithful with a few things, I will put you in charge of many things; enter into the joy of your master."
MATTHEW 25:23

Please help my grandchild to be faithful with the talents you give them. Help them to use their skills for your glory and honor.

Day 6

She looks well to the ways of her household, and does not eat the bread of idleness.
PROVERBS 31:24

The woman in Proverbs 31 was not idle, she was creative and made the most of her time. Please help my grandchild to not be wasteful with the time and capabilities you have given to them. Let them not fill their days with empty things that take away from their success and service to you.

Day 7

Do you see a man skilled in his work? He will stand before kings; He will not stand before obscure men.

Proverbs 22:29

As my grandchild grows, help them to refine their talents and complete tasks well. Bless them with a good reputation when it comes to the quality of their work.

God has given you some great talents and abilities...

_____

_____

_____

_____

_____

_____

_____

_____

You are so unique. Your worth is priceless!

_____

_____

_____

_____

_____

_____

_____

_____

_____

_____

_____

_____

Week 27

Favor upon Favor

Favor:

KIND REGARD; SUPPORT; DEFENSE; VINDICATION; OR
DISPOSITION TO AID, BEFRIEND, SUPPORT, PROMOTE OR
JUSTIFY

Day 1

But Noah found favor in the eyes of the LORD.

GENESIS 6:8

Lord, please look upon my grandchild with grace and mercy just as you did with Noah and his family.

Day 2

The LORD make His face shine on you, and be gracious to you; the LORD lift up His countenance on you, and give you peace.

NUMBERS 6:25-26

I pray this blessing over my grandchild. Let your face shine on them with favor. Guide them through life and give them the true peace that only comes from you.

Day 3

Do not store up for yourselves treasures on earth, where moth and rust destroy, and where thieves break in and steal. But store up for yourselves treasures in heaven, where neither moth nor rust destroys, and where thieves do not break in or steal; for where your treasure is, there your heart will be also…

MATTHEW 6:19-21

Please help my grandchild to favor the things of Heaven and not Earth. Help them to set their mind and heart upon you Jesus.

Day 4

For the LORD God is a sun and shield; the LORD gives grace and glory; no good thing does He withhold from those who walk uprightly.

PSALM 84:11

You are my grandchild's guide and protector; their sun and shield. Thank you that you bestow favor and honor. Help them to walk with you so that they will not miss out on the many good things you have in store.

Day 5

Do not let kindness and truth leave you; bind them around your neck, write them on the tablet of your heart. So you will find favor and good repute in the sight of God and man.

PROVERBS 3:3-4

As my grandchild follows and honors you, please give them favor in the sight of those they interact with. Help them to be adored, liked and admired by many.

Day 6

The LORD said to Moses, "I will also do this thing of which you have spoken; for you have found favor in My sight and I have known you by name."

EXODUS 33:17

Father, you know my grandchild by name. Help them to grow very close to you and speak with you on a first name basis.

Day 7

Bless the LORD, O my soul, and all that is within me, bless His holy name. Bless the LORD, O my soul, and forget none of His benefits; who pardons all your iniquities, who heals all your diseases; who redeems your life from the pit, who crowns you with lovingkindness and compassion; who satisfies your years with good things, so that your youth is renewed like the eagle.

PSALM 103:1-5

Thank you for being such an amazing God. You forgive, heal, redeem and satisfy our desires. Please have favor toward my grandchild and let them experience your goodness in the ways this passage describes.

I am praying that God will give you favor in these areas...

_____

_____

_____

_____

_____

_____

Authentic Joy

Joy :

THE PASSION OR EMOTION EXCITED BY THE ACQUISITION OR
EXPECTATION OF GOOD

Day 1

A joyful heart makes a cheerful face, but when the heart is sad, the spirit is broken.

PROVERBS 15:13

Help my grandchild to have a cheerful disposition. I pray that you will help them follow your ways to avoid the heartache that comes from disobedience. At times when they do experience sadness, please bring them comfort.

Day 2

Light is sown like seed for the righteous and gladness for the upright in heart.

PSALM 97:11

Please help my grandchild to experience the joy that comes from making decisions based on following your truths in the Bible. Let their heart be glad because they are following you with their life.

Day 3

For I have come to have much joy and comfort in your love, because the hearts of the saints have been refreshed through you, brother.

PHILEMON 1:7

Paul was joyful in his heart because of Philemon's attitude. Let my grandchild be a refreshing presence and a blessing as they bring joy to others through their attitude and actions.

Day 4

The hope of the righteous is gladness, but the expectation of the wicked perishes.
PROVERBS 10:28

Thank you that our eternity in Heaven will be full of joy. Put the hope of Heaven into the heart of my grandchild. Help them to know that true joy comes from knowing you.

Day 5

Rejoice in the Lord always; again I will say, rejoice!
PHILIPPIANS 4:4

There is nothing more valuable in life than experiencing the contentment that comes from knowing Jesus. Help my grandchild to know that lifelong joy can only come from serving you Lord.

Day 6

This is the day which the LORD has made; let us rejoice and be glad in it.
PSALM 118:24

Help my grandchild to find joy in each day because each day is a gift from you. Let them live to the fullest with thanksgiving.

Day 7

…rejoicing in hope, persevering in tribulation, devoted to prayer…
ROMANS 12:12

Help my grandchild to have patience and draw close to you in trials. Let them be faithful in prayer and not lose the hope and joy that comes from knowing God's unexplainable peace and faithful presence.

You bring joy to my life...

_____

_____

_____

_____

_____

_____

_____

_____

_____

_____

_____

_____

_____

_____

PLACE
PICTURE OVER
FRAME

PLACE
PICTURE OVER
FRAME

Kind and Compassionate

Kind:

PROCEEDING FROM TENDERNESS OR GOODNESS OF HEART

Compassion:

HAVING A HEART THAT IS TENDER AND EASILY MOVED BY THE
DISTRESSES, SUFFERINGS,
WANTS AND INFIRMITIES OF OTHERS

Day 1

So, as those who have been chosen of God, holy and beloved, put on a heart of compassion, kindness, humility, gentleness and patience…

COLOSSIANS 3:12

Thank you Father that my grandchild is your chosen one. It is comforting to know that you love this child dearly. I pray that you will develop a kind and compassionate heart within them.

Day 2

Be kind to one another, tender-hearted, forgiving each other, just as God in Christ also has forgiven you.

EPHESIANS 4:32

Help my grandchild to recognize that they are forgiven by you Jesus. Lead them to see the depth of your kindness and compassion, and help them to extend that toward others.

Day 3

…A man was going down from Jerusalem to Jericho, and fell among robbers, and they stripped him and beat him, and went away leaving him half dead. And by chance a priest was going down on that road, and when he saw him, he passed by on the other side. Likewise a Levite also, when he came to the place and saw him, passed by on the other side. But a Samaritan, who was on a journey, came upon him; and when he saw him, he felt compassion, and came to him and bandaged up his wounds…and took care of him.

LUKE 10:30-34

Just as the Samaritan had a kind and compassionate heart, help my grandchild to notice and not ignore those in need. Motivate them to take action and be your ministering servant.

137

Day 4

To sum up, all of you be harmonious, sympathetic, brotherly, kindhearted and humble in spirit; not returning evil for evil or insult for insult, but giving a blessing instead; for you were called for the very purpose that you might inherit a blessing.

1 PETER 3:8-9

Only with your assistance can we live this way. Please work in the heart of my grandchild. Let them be compassionate toward those who are difficult to love. Show them your perspective and how to act in a Christ honoring way. Please bless them as they do this.

Day 5

A righteous man has regard for the life of his animal, but even the compassion of the wicked is cruel.

PROVERBS 12:10

Help my grandchild to grow up with a love for your creation. Instill in them a desire to honor what you have made and to treat animals with respect and care.

Day 6

One who is gracious to a poor man lends to the LORD, and He will repay him for his good deed.

PROVERBS 19:17

Help my grandchild to have concern toward those who do not have many possessions. With an attitude of kindness, may they give as if they were giving to you Lord. Please reward them because of their compassion.

Day 7

Thus has the LORD of hosts said, "Dispense true justice and practice kindness and compassion each to his brother; and do not oppress the widow or the orphan, the stranger or the poor; and do not devise evil in your hearts against one another."

ZECHARIAH 7:9-10

Please let my grandchild care about those who are lonely and in need. Help them to be quick in showing compassion toward people who are often ignored.

A little kindness goes a long way...

_____

_____

_____

_____

_____

_____

_____

_____

Week 30

Enduring Patience

Patience:

THE SUFFERING OF AFFLICTIONS, PAIN, TOIL, CALAMITY, PROVOCATION OR OTHER EVIL WITH A CALM UNRUFFLED TEMPER; ENDURANCE WITHOUT MURMURING FRETFULNESS. THE ACT OR QUALITY OF WAITING LONG FOR JUSTICE OR EXPECTED GOOD WITHOUT DISCONTENT.

Day 1

He who is slow to anger has great understanding, but he who is quick-tempered exalts folly.
PROVERBS 14:29

Help my grandchild to hold their tongue and temper. Let them realize the importance of fully evaluating a situation first, instead of lashing out and regretting what was said or done. Please give them patience in their interactions with others.

Day 2

The end of a matter is better than its beginning; patience of spirit is better than haughtiness of spirit.
ECCLESIASTES 7:8

Give my grandchild the grace to finish what they start and to do thorough work with projects. Let them avoid doing poor work and help them not to quit because of impatience. When they do something well, guard their heart from pride.

Day 3

Rest in the LORD and wait patiently for Him; do not fret because of him who prospers in his way, because of the man who carries out wicked schemes.
PSALM 37:7

When my grandchild comes before you with requests, help them to realize that you have good plans even if there are not immediate answers. Help them to give their worries to you and to wait for your answer with patience. Thank you for bringing about your good plans and justice in your perfect timing.

Day 4

You too be patient; strengthen your hearts, for the coming of the Lord is near.

JAMES 5:8

As this world gets crazier and my grandchild sees the scary things going on around them, give them strength to stand firm and patiently wait for you. Help them to look forward to Heaven and to the possibility that you may come back in their lifetime.

Day 5

I wait for the LORD, my soul does wait, and in His word do I hope.

PSALM 130:5

Some attend to their own pursuits without waiting for you. Instead, help my grandchild to seek your guidance and devote themselves to waiting for your answer and direction. Give them hope because your word and promises can be trusted.

Day 6

We urge you, brethren, admonish the unruly, encourage the fainthearted, help the weak, be patient with everyone.

1 THESSALONIANS 5:14

Sometimes my grandchild will encounter difficult people in various situations. Help them to handle these interactions with grace and patience.

Day 7

Now you followed my teaching, conduct, purpose, faith, patience, love, perseverance...
2 TIMOTHY 3:10

Lord, to have a way of life that includes faith, love, endurance and patience on a daily basis is admirable and can only happen with your intervention. Please guide my grandchild toward these qualities as they learn about their purpose in your kingdom and who they are in Christ.

Patience is difficult. I am praying that you will have patience...

_____

_____

_____

_____

_____

_____

_____

There was a time when I had to be really patient...

Week 31

A Person of Generosity

Generosity:

THE QUALITY OF BEING GENEROUS; LIBERALITY IN PRINCIPLE;
A DISPOSITION TO GIVE LIBERALLY OR TO BESTOW FAVORS

Day 1

Now this I say, he who sows sparingly will also reap sparingly, and he who sows bountifully will also reap bountifully.

2 CORINTHIANS 9:6

Lord, please work in my grandchild's heart, help them to be a generous person and to give when the need arises. Let them not hesitate to lavish blessings on other people.

Day 2

Instruct those who are rich in this present world not to be conceited or to fix their hope on the uncertainty of riches, but on God, who richly supplies us with all things to enjoy. Instruct them to do good, to be rich in good works, to be generous and ready to share…

1 TIMOTHY 6:17-18

You ask us to hope in you and not in wealth because it is uncertain. You are the one who has given us all we have and everything that is enjoyable. Help my grandchild to understand this and be rich in generosity.

Day 3

But when you give to the poor, do not let your left hand know what your right hand is doing, so that your giving will be in secret; and your Father who sees what is done in secret will reward you.

MATTHEW 6:3-4

Help my grandchild to have pure intentions when giving and to enjoy anonymous acts of generosity without the need to get credit. As they bless others, it blesses you and your rewards are good!

Day 4

"The silver is Mine and the gold is Mine," declares the LORD of hosts.
HAGGAI 2:08

Help my grandchild to see that all financial resources are yours. Let them realize that you will provide everything they need when they put you first and trust you.

Day 5

We know love by this, that He laid down His life for us; and we ought to lay down our lives for the brethren. But whoever has the world's goods, and sees his brother in need and closes his heart against him, how does the love of God abide in him? Little children, let us not love with word or with tongue, but in deed and truth.
1 JOHN 3:16-18

Please bless my grandchild with a spirit of generosity. Help them to care for people who are in need and take notice of how they can help others. Let them experience joy in serving others.

Day 6

And He [Jesus] looked up and saw the rich putting their gifts into the treasury. And He saw a poor widow putting in two small copper coins. And He said, "Truly I say to you, this poor widow put in more than all of them; for they all out of their surplus put into the offering; but she out of her poverty put in all that she had to live on."
LUKE 21:1-4

Like the widow in this verse, please help my grandchild not to stop tithing in the difficult times. Let them learn that you will be faithful to provide, even in the seasons when money may not be abundant.

Day 7

Each one must do just as he has purposed in his heart, not grudgingly or under compulsion, for God loves a cheerful giver.

2 CORINTHIANS 9:7

Please help my grandchild not to be attached to possessions or money. Help them not to idolize the material things of this world. In this way, let them be generous with their funds and cheerful with giving. Also, please give them discernment with how much they should give. Help them to find balance with helping others and also taking care of their own needs and their future family's needs.

Thoughts about generosity...

_____

_____

_____

_____

_____

_____

_____

_____

Some ideas about how to be generous and how to serve...

Week 32

God's Dependable Provision

Provision:

Things provided; preparation; measures taken before hand

Day 1

Honor the LORD from your wealth and from the first of all your produce; so your barns will be filled with plenty and your vats will overflow with new wine.

PROVERBS 3:9-10

Lord please help my grandchild to honor you with their money and how they give. When they take that step of faith, please provide for them.

Day 2

Now Abraham was old, advanced in age; and the Lord had blessed Abraham in every way.

GENESIS 24:1

Like Abraham, will you please bless my grandchild in every way? Please give them a full healthy life while supplying all that they need.

Day 3

Look at the birds of the air, that they do not sow, nor reap nor gather into barns, and yet your heavenly Father feeds them. Are you not worth much more than they?

MATTHEW 6:26

Thank you that you care about every need, big and small. Help my grandchild to understand how valuable they are to you.

Day 4

For He has satisfied the parched soul,
And the hungry soul He has filled with what is good.

PSALM 107:9

Help my grandchild to know that you will reach out and satisfy the deepest needs of the human heart. You can take their brokenness and make them whole. You can fill the voids in their life with your presence. Let my grandchild know that you are able to provide all spiritual blessings and give them hope and joy about the future.

Day 5

And my God will supply all your needs according to His riches in glory in Christ Jesus.

PHILIPPIANS 4:19

Thank you Jesus that you can meet every physical, emotional, financial and spiritual need. Help my grandchild to realize this and turn to you for security, safety and stability.

Day 6

If you then, being evil, know how to give good gifts to your children, how much more will your Father who is in heaven give what is good to those who ask Him!

MATTHEW 7:11

I love my grandchild so much. Thank you Lord for exceeding our greatest human efforts of care and love because you are a perfect Heavenly Father! Thank you for taking care of my grandchild. Give them good things as you see fit.

Day 7

Do not worry then, saying, 'What will we eat?' or 'What will we drink?' or 'What will we wear for clothing?' For the Gentiles eagerly seek all these things; for your Heavenly Father knows that you need all these things.

MATTHEW 6:31-32

I don't know the future, but I know you are faithful. If money is tight, thank you that you know all of my grandchild's needs and will provide. Help me to trust you with my grandchild and rest all worries in your capable hands.

I see God's provision in your life...

_____

_____

_____

_____

_____

_____

_____

_____

Acknowledgment of God's Greatness

Great:

CHIEF; OF VAST POWER AND EXCELLENCE; SUPREME;
ILLUSTRIOUS; AS THE GREAT GOD; THE GREAT CREATOR

Day 1

Let them praise the name of the LORD, for He commanded and they were created.
PSALM 148:5

Out of your power, all of creation came to exist through your word and command. I praise you God that my grandchild came into being with their individual qualities, because of your will.

Day 2

Behold, I am the LORD, the God of all flesh; is anything too difficult for Me?
JEREMIAH 32:27

God, you are so excellent and great, there is nothing too hard for you. Please help my grandchild to understand this and get a glimpse of how mighty and extraordinary you are.

Day 3

I kept looking until thrones were set up, and the Ancient of Days took His seat; His vesture was like white snow and the hair of His head like pure wool. His throne was ablaze with flames, its wheels were a burning fire.
DANIEL 7:9

...His dominion is an everlasting dominion which will not pass away; and His kingdom is one which will not be destroyed.
DANIEL 7:14

You are referred to as the Ancient of Days. You are most holy and glorious. Help my grandchild to know that you are the author of time and the all powerful God who is to be revered and honored.

Day 4

The LORD utters His voice before His army; surely His camp is very great, for strong is He who carries out His word. The day of the LORD is indeed great and very awesome, and who can endure it?

JOEL 2:11

Help my grandchild to know that the King of the Universe is by their side, ready to help with anything they need. Thank you that you are true to your word and your promises.

Day 5

For behold, He who forms mountains and creates the wind and declares to man what are His thoughts, He who makes dawn into darkness and treads on the high places of the earth, the LORD God of hosts is His name.

AMOS 4:13

All of creation is subject to your authority. Help my grandchild to realize the depth and breadth of your power and greatness. Help them to submit to you.

Day 6

Bless the LORD, O my soul! O LORD my God, You are very great; You are clothed with splendor and majesty…

PSALM 104:1

Help my grandchild to praise you because of your importance and excellence. Let them understand that they serve a God full of splendor and majesty. The Almighty God, with all dominion and control over the entire universe.

Day 7

...I saw the Lord sitting on a throne, lofty and exalted, with the train of His
robe filling the temple.

ISAIAH 6:1

*You are the one true King, excellent and glorious. You are great, holy and worthy
of praise. Help my grandchild to give you the honor that you deserve by
following you with their life.*

Nature speaks of God's greatness...

PLACE
PICTURE OVER
FRAME

PLACE
PICTURE OVER
FRAME

Week 34

The Peace of Christ

Peace:

FREEDOM FROM AGITATION OR DISTURBANCE BY THE PASSIONS, AS FROM FEAR, TERROR, ANGER, ANXIETY OR THE LIKE; QUIETNESS OF MIND; TRANQUILITY; CALMNESS; QUIET OF CONSCIENCE

Day 1

He must turn away from evil and do good; he must seek peace and purse it.

1 PETER 3:11

Father, help my grandchild to be a peace seeker and pursuer of what is right. Help them to readily confess sin and make honorable choices.

Day 2

Deceit is in the heart of those who devise evil, but counselors of peace have joy.

PROVERBS 12:20

Help my grandchild to promote peace in their relationships and interactions with others. Let them bring your presence and your joy into the conversations that they have with other people.

Day 3

Be anxious for nothing, but in everything by prayer and supplication with thanksgiving let your requests be made known to God. And the peace of God, which surpasses all comprehension, will guard your hearts and your minds in Christ Jesus.

PHILIPPIANS 4:6-7

In some circumstances it is very easy to be anxious. Please help my grandchild to be quick to ask you for help. Let your peace flood their heart and mind as they trust in you. Quiet their soul and provide them with rest.

Day 4

Now may the Lord of peace Himself continually grant you peace in every circumstance. The Lord be with you all!

2 THESSALONIANS 3:16

You are the Lord of peace. Please let your Spirit rest on my grandchild and help them to be at peace in all times and in every way. Let the peace of Jesus be a constant source, surrounding their heart and mind.

Day 5

Therefore, beloved, since you look for these things, be diligent to be found by Him in peace, spotless and blameless...

2 PETER 3:14

The most important part of life is to be at peace with God. Please help my grandchild to be at peace with you Jesus and have peace in their heart because of the security that is found in you.

Day 6

But the wisdom from above is first pure, then peaceable, gentle, reasonable, full of mercy and good fruits, unwavering, without hypocrisy.

JAMES 3:17

A component of true wisdom is a desire and love for peace. Please help my grandchild to be wise and realize that stirring up strife is not from you. Help them to desire to be at peace with others.

Day 7

And He got up and rebuked the wind and said to the sea, "Hush, be still." And the wind died down and it became perfectly calm. And He said to them, "Why are you afraid?
Do you still have no faith?"

MARK 4:39-40

Jesus, you can calm physical storms that come and you also calm the storms in our hearts and lives. Please do this for my grandchild and bring them your peace and rest when they are in need. Help them to have peace because of their faith in you.

May you experience the peace of Christ in your heart...

_____

_____

_____

_____

_____

_____

_____

_____

Verses for when you feel anxious or worried...

_____

_____

_____

_____

_____

_____

_____

_____

_____

_____

_____

_____

_____

Week 35

Thankfulness

Thankful:

EXPRESSION OF GRATITUDE; ACKNOWLEDGMENT OF A FAVOR

Day 1

Let the peace of Christ rule in your hearts, to which indeed you were called in one body;
and be thankful.

COLOSSIANS 3:15

Father, I ask that your peace will rule in the heart of my grandchild. Help them to be content with what they have and not feel the need to get more possessions. Instead may they be filled with thanksgiving.

Day 2

Let us come before His presence with thanksgiving, let us shout joyfully to Him with psalms.
For the LORD is a great God and a great King above all gods…

PSALM 95:2-3

You deserve to be acknowledged and praised because you are great and worthy. Help my grandchild to approach you with thankfulness for all you have done.

Day 3

…in everything give thanks; for this is God's will for you in Christ Jesus.

1 THESSALONIANS 5:18

When difficult times come, sometimes it is very hard to see anything positive. You ask that we give thanks for everything because it is your will. Help my grandchild to know deep down in their soul that you are working in their life for their good throughout all situations.

Day 4

Then He took the five loaves and the two fish, and looking up to heaven, He blessed them, and broke them, and kept giving them to the disciples to set before the people.

Luke 9:16

Just like you provided food for a hungry crowd, you give us food on a daily basis. Help my grandchild not to neglect thanking you for food before meals. Let them carry a thankful attitude throughout the entire day.

Day 5

I will give thanks to the LORD with all my heart; I will tell of all Your wonders.

PSALM 9:1

Sometimes God, you work in miraculous ways and do great things for us. As my grandchild experiences your mercies and wonderful deeds, help them not to forget to thank you for your blessings. As they walk through life with you, let them remember all you have done on their behalf.

Day 6

Now one of them, when he saw that he had been healed, turned back, glorifying God with a loud voice…

LUKE 17:15

Sometimes we forget to say thank you after you do something amazing. Help my grandchild not to forget your blessings and give them a desire to draw close to you with a heart of thanksgiving.

Day 7

Enter His gates with thanksgiving and His courts with praise. Give thanks to Him, bless His name. For the LORD is good; His lovingkindness is everlasting and His faithfulness to all generations.

PSALM 100: 4-5

When my grandchild goes to church, help them to learn more about how powerful you are and what you have done for them. Help them to be thankful for your faithfulness.

I am so incredibly thankful for you...

_____

_____

_____

_____

_____

_____

_____

_____

_____

Week 36

A Humble Heart

Humility:

FREEDOM FROM PRIDE AND ARROGANCE; HUMBLENESS OF MIND

Day 1

The reward of humility and the fear of the Lord are riches, honor and life.
PROVERBS 22:4

Help my grandchild to humble themselves before you, acknowledging you are to be respected and honored. Bless them with riches and a good life as they make moral choices out of humility.

Day 2

But he who boasts is to boast in the Lord. For it is not he who commends himself that is approved, but he whom the Lord commends.
2 CORINTHIANS 10:17-18

All good things, joyful circumstances and any talents or achievements come from you Lord. Please help my grandchild to keep a humble heart no matter how successful they may become. Let them realize that they are successful only because of your intervention.

Day 3

Do nothing from selfishness or empty conceit, but with humility of mind regard one another as more important than yourselves; do not merely look out for your own personal interests, but also for the interests of others.
PHILIPPIANS 2:3-4

Give my grandchild the perspective of humility as they interact with others. Let their attitude be like you Jesus. Strengthen them with patience and love and please show them how to care for people.

Day 4

Who among you is wise and understanding? Let him show by his good behavior his deeds in the gentleness of wisdom.

JAMES 3:13

Out of a humble heart, help my grandchild implement good deeds with the purpose of blessing others. Make them wise with your principles.

Day 5

Therefore humble yourselves under the mighty hand of God, that He may exalt you at the proper time…

1 PETER 5:6

It is good to know that when we humble our hearts before you Lord, you will lift us up and encourage us. Your hand is mighty and able to do many things. Please help my grandchild to understand this.

Day 6

For through the grace given to me I say to everyone among you not to think more highly of himself than he ought to think; but to think so as to have sound judgment, as God has allotted to each a measure of faith.

ROMANS 12:3

Help my grandchild to refrain from boasting and bragging about accomplishments or possessions. In the light of your excellence and your mercy, help them to think of themselves with sober judgment.

Day 7

Be of the same mind toward one another; do not be haughty in mind, but associate with the lowly. Do not be wise in your own estimation.

ROMANS 12:16

Help my grandchild to be willing to befriend people that may not be the most popular. Let them serve with humility due to their realization of your grace Lord. Show them opportunities where they can go the extra mile to serve someone in need.

PLACE
PICTURE OVER
FRAME

Having humility takes a lot of courage...

Week 37

Diligent Obedience

Obedient:

SUBMISSIVE TO AUTHORITY; YIELDING COMPLIANCE WITH COMMANDS, ORDERS OR INJUNCTIONS; PERFORMING WHAT IS REQUIRED OR ABSTAINING FROM WHAT IS FORBID

Day 1

As obedient children, do not be conformed to the former lusts
which were yours in your ignorance.

1 PETER 1:14

As you transform my grandchild's heart, help them conform to your ways and not get pulled into evil desires or worldly behavior. Instead, let their allegiance and obedience rest in you Lord.

Day 2

For this reason also, since the day we heard of it, we have not ceased to pray for you and to ask that you may be filled with the knowledge of His will in all spiritual wisdom and understanding, so that you will walk in a manner worthy of the Lord, to please Him in all respects, bearing fruit in every good work and increasing in the knowledge of God...

COLOSSIANS 1:9-10

I pray that my grandchild will obey you. Give them an understanding of your will so that they can live a life that is worthy of you Lord. Let their love for Jesus be evident in their character and deeds.

Day 3

I will put My Spirit within you and cause you to walk in My statutes, and you will be careful to observe My ordinances.

EZEKIEL 36:27

Lord, it is the work of your Spirit that actually moves us to obey your commands. Impress right and wrong on my grandchild's heart and help them make right choices.

Day 4

I have no greater joy than this, to hear of my children walking in the truth.

3 JOHN 1:4

Truly there is no greater joy than knowing that my grandchild has the opportunity to walk with Jesus. Please guide them toward you and help them to walk in truth.

Day 5

You shall therefore love the Lord your God, and always keep His charge, His statutes, His ordinances, and His commandments.

DEUTERONOMY 11:1

The Israelites were blessed when they followed you. I pray that my grandchild will love you always and live obediently. Help them to follow your commands and seek out forgiveness when they make a poor choice.

Day 6

We are destroying speculations and every lofty thing raised up against the knowledge of God, and we are taking every thought captive to the obedience of Christ...

2 Corinthians 10:5

Sometimes thoughts can be disobedient to you Lord. Please help my grandchild to learn how to take their thoughts captive and make them obedient to Christ. Let them guard what their eyes see and ears hear.

Day 7

Children, obey your parents in the Lord, for this is right. Honor your father and mother (which is the first commandment with a promise), so that it may be well with you, and that you may live long on the Earth.

EPHESIANS 6:1-3

Please help my grandchild to obey their parents. Help their parents to set appropriate guidelines and rules for my grandchild so that they can grow up to follow you and be an honorable person. Help my grandchild to obey you Jesus. Bless them because of their obedience.

Specific ways I'm praying for your family...

_____

_____

_____

_____

_____

_____

_____

Week 38

Faithfulness

Faithful:

FIRMLY ADHERING TO DUTY; OF TRUE FIDELITY; LOYAL; TRUE TO ALLEGIANCE

Day 1

Samuel said to the people, "Do not fear. You have committed all this evil, yet do not turn aside from following the LORD, but serve the LORD with all your heart."

1 SAMUEL 12:20

Father, you are faithful. When we make mistakes you want us to come back and experience your forgiveness and grace. Help my grandchild to understand the depth of your mercy and faithfulness to them.

Day 2

This I recall to my mind, therefore I have hope. The Lord's lovingkindnesses indeed never cease, for His compassions never fail. They are new every morning; great is Your faithfulness. "The Lord is my portion," says my soul, "Therefore I have hope in Him." The Lord is good to those who wait for Him, to the person who seeks Him. It is good that he waits silently for the salvation of the Lord.

LAMENTATIONS 3:21-26

Lord, you have unfailing compassion toward us. I ask that my grandchild will come to know you as their faithful God. Help them to put their hope and trust in you.

Day 3

This command I entrust to you, Timothy, my son, in accordance with the prophecies previously made concerning you, that by them you fight the good fight, keeping faith and a good conscience, which some have rejected and suffered shipwreck in regard to their faith.

1 TIMOTHY 1:18-19

Help my grandchild to stay faithful to you. Help them to hold on to their convictions. Out of a clear conscience, let them make godly decisions so that their faith will remain strong.

178

Day 4

So you shall observe to do just as the LORD your God has commanded you; you shall not turn aside to the right or to the left. You shall walk in all the way which the Lord your God has commanded you, that you may live and that it may be well with you, and that you may prolong your days in the land which you will possess.

DEUTERONOMY 5:32-33

Let my grandchild walk with you on the straight path and not stray to the right or left. Help them to reap the spiritual and physical blessings that come with obedience to you Lord.

Day 5

Paul, an apostle of Christ Jesus by the will of God, to the saints who are at Ephesus and who are faithful in Christ Jesus…

EPHESIANS 1:1

The people in Ephesus were known for their faithfulness to Jesus. Help my grandchild to be known for their faithfulness as well. Let them have a reputation that is God honoring.

Day 6

Know therefore that the Lord your God, He is God, the faithful God, who keeps His covenant and His lovingkindness to a thousandth generation with those who love Him and keep His commandments…

DEUTERONOMY 7:9

You are God, faithful toward those who follow your word. Help my grandchild to experience your incredible faithfulness in many ways throughout their life.

Day 7

Therefore let him who thinks he stands take heed that he does not fall. No temptation has overtaken you but such as is common to man; and God is faithful, who will not allow you to be tempted beyond what you are able, but with the temptation will provide the way of escape also, so that you will be able to endure it.

1 CORINTHIANS 10:12-13

When various temptations come, help my grandchild to stand firm and guard their heart and eyes. Give them the wisdom to avoid situations that encourage temptation. Please protect them from overwhelming enticements and provide escapes so that they can overcome any evil. Thank you for your faithfulness in this.

God is faithful and trustworthy. I've seen this in many ways...

_____

_____

_____

_____

_____

_____

_____

Week 39

God's Help

Help:

TO AID; TO ASSIST; TO LEND STRENGTH OR MEANS TOWARD
EFFECTING A PURPOSE

Day 1

In my trouble I cried to the LORD, and He answered me.
PSALM 120:1

Thank you for answering if my grandchild calls out to you in distress, you are always reliable. Help my grandchild to know that whenever they need help they can call on you.

Day 2

For by their own sword they did not possess the land, and their own arm did not save them, but Your right hand and Your arm and the light of Your presence, for You favored them.
PSALM 44:3

Any accomplishments or victories that my grandchild may experience are because of your help. Out of love for them, you will enable them to be successful. Out of a grateful heart, help them to recognize your work on their behalf.

Day 3

Trust in the LORD with all your heart and do not lean on your own understanding. In all your ways acknowledge Him, and He will make your paths straight.
PROVERBS 3:6

Lord, you promise that if we submit to you, clarity will come and you will direct our path. As my grandchild grows to trust you and accept your direction, guide them through life.

Day 4

God is our refuge and strength, a very present help in trouble. Therefore we will not fear, though the earth should change and though the mountains slip into the heart of the sea…
PSALM 46:1-2

Please help my grandchild to have a solid understanding of who you are. Be their refuge, strength and a present help at all times. Help them to grow in their trust and knowledge of you.

Day 5

Behold, God is my helper; the Lord is the sustainer of my soul.
PSALM 54:4

You are our help, the one that sustains us. Let my grandchild rely on you for what they need, especially on days when they are weary or in situations that seem impossible.

Day 6

Though I walk in the midst of trouble, You will revive me; You will stretch forth Your hand against the wrath of my enemies, and Your right hand will save me.
PSALM 138:7

Troubles will come but thank you that you are my grandchild's faithful protector. Please save them from disaster and preserve their life. Thank you that you revive us when discouragement comes and that you are a shelter for my grandchild at all times.

Day 7

He sent from on high, He took me; He drew me out of many waters. He delivered me from my strong enemy, and from those who hated me, for they were too mighty for me. They confronted me in the day of my calamity, but the Lord was my stay. He brought me forth also into a broad place; He rescued me, because He delighted in me.

PSALM 18:16-19

There are going to be days when my grandchild encounters dangerous people or scary situations. Thank you that you are their protector and Savior. Place your faithful hand of mercy on them. I ask that your favor will rest on them and that they will be your delight.

I'm praying that God will help you with...

_____

_____

_____

_____

_____

_____

_____

Week 40

Assurance of God's Promises

Promise:

In Scripture, the promise of God is the declaration or assurance which God has given in his word of bestowing blessings on his people. Such assurance resting on the perfect justice, power, benevolence and immutable veracity of God, cannot fail of performance

Day 1

This is the promise which He Himself made to us: eternal life.

1 JOHN 2:25

Thank you Lord for the most assuring promise of all, that if we accept Jesus, we will live with you forever in Heaven. Help my grandchild to hold this promise in their heart throughout their entire life.

Day 2

The words of the LORD are pure words; silver tried in a furnace on the earth, refined seven times.

PSALM 12:6

Your words Lord are true and flawless. Your promises are genuine. Help my grandchild to know that you mean what you say.

Day 3

I will instruct you and teach you in the way which you should go; I will counsel you with My eye upon you. Do not be as the horse or as the mule which have no understanding, whose trappings include bit and bridle to hold them in check, otherwise they will not come near to you.

PSALM 32:8-9

Please instruct my grandchild in the right path. Teach and counsel them in the way they should go. Thank you that you have your hand of guidance on their life. Help them to follow your plans willingly.

Day 4

For as high as the heavens are above the earth, so great is His lovingkindness toward those who fear Him. As far as the east is from the west, so far has
He removed our transgressions from us.
PSALM 103:11-12

Thank you Jesus that you promise to remove our sins completely. Please help my grandchild to believe this truth when they make mistakes. Help them to know your forgiveness is a promise that you will keep.

Day 5

Come to Me, all who are weary and heavy-laden, and I will give you rest. Take My yoke upon you and learn from Me, for I am gentle and humble in heart,
and you will find rest for your souls.
MATTHEW 11:28-29

Thank you for your promise of rest if we place ourselves in your care. Please help my grandchild to know the peace that comes from following you and committing their life to you.

Day 6

He will cover you with His pinions, and under His wings you may seek refuge; His faithfulness is a shield and bulwark. You will not be afraid of the terror by night, or of the arrow that flies by day; of the pestilence that stalks in darkness, or of the destruction that lays waste at noon.
PSALM 91:4-6

Thank you for your promises of protection and refuge. Thank you that you will be a faithful shield around my grandchild and that they have nothing to fear because you are actively guarding them.

Day 7

But He said, "The things that are impossible with people are possible with God."
LUKE 18:27

Help my grandchild to know that even in impossible situations, when it is hard to trust your promises, you are working behind the scenes because nothing is impossible with you.

I'm praying these promises from God over you...

_____

_____

_____

_____

_____

_____

_____

_____

Some special things I enjoy doing with you include...

PLACE
PICTURE OVER
FRAME

PLACE
PICTURE OVER
FRAME

PLACE
PICTURE OVER
FRAME

PLACE
PICTURE OVER
FRAME

When I was your age...

_____
_____
_____
_____
_____
_____
_____
_____
_____
_____
_____
_____

PLACE
PICTURE OVER
FRAME

PLACE
PICTURE OVER
FRAME

PLACE
PICTURE OVER
FRAME

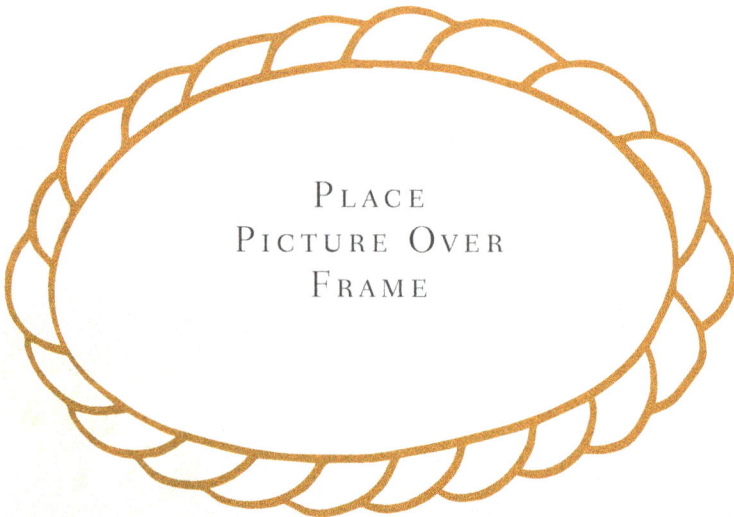

PLACE
PICTURE OVER
FRAME

Here are a few stories I want to share with you...

PLACE
PICTURE OVER
FRAME

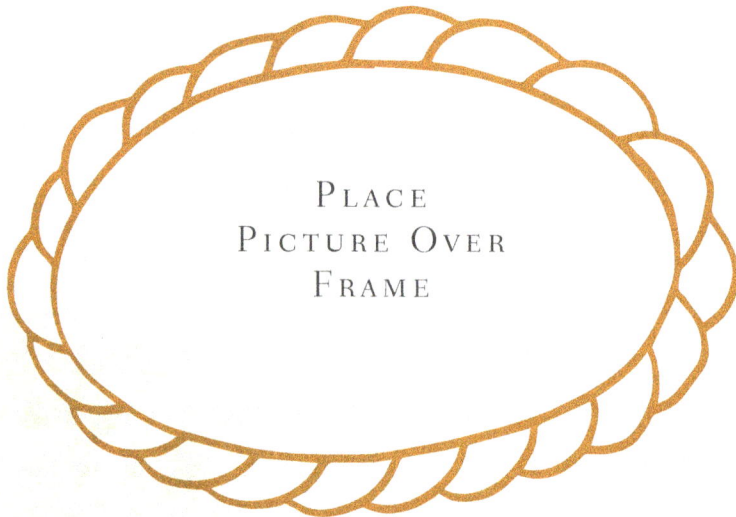

PLACE
PICTURE OVER
FRAME

Some family history to share...

PLACE
PICTURE OVER
FRAME

PLACE
PICTURE OVER
FRAME

PLACE
PICTURE OVER
FRAME

PLACE
PICTURE OVER
FRAME

I am so proud of you...

I want you to always remember...

_____

_____

_____

_____

_____

_____

_____

_____

_____

_____

_____

_____

PLACE
PICTURE OVER
FRAME

PLACE
PICTURE OVER
FRAME

PLACE
PICTURE OVER
FRAME

PLACE
PICTURE OVER
FRAME

The Lord bless _____ and keep you;
The Lord make His face shine on you,
and be gracious to you;
The Lord lift up His countenance on you,
And give you peace.

NUMBERS 6:24-26

A Grandparent's Devotional- Close to My Heart: 40 Weeks of Scripture, Prayer and Reflection for Your Grandchild
ISBN 978-1-7344708-1-9 HARDCOVER EDITION
© 2020 by Rebekah Tague
Scripture quotations taken from the New American Standard Bible® (NASB),
Copyright © 1960, 1962, 1963, 1968, 1971, 1972, 1973,
1975, 1977, 1995 by The Lockman Foundation
Used by permission. www.Lockman.org

Dictionary quotations taken from: Webster, Noah. An American Dictionary of the English Language : Intended to Exhibit, I. The Origin, Affinities and Primary Signification of English Words, As Far As They Have Been Ascertained; II. the Genuine Orthography and Pronunciation of Words, According to General. S. Converse, Printed by Hezekiah Howe, 1828.
Copyright: Public Domain

All photography is the property of Rebekah Tague
Questions? Comments? Please write to prayerlegacybooks@gmail.com

This book is dedicated to some VERY SPECIAL grandparents:
Mima and Grandpa
Papa
Tita
You are deeply loved and we are incredibly thankful to have you in our lives! Thank you for praying for your grandkids!
And also this book is dedicated in loving memory to grandparents
Grandpa Glenn and Grandma Edith and Grandma Sandy: We miss you so much. Your legacy of blessing continues. We are all really looking forward to seeing you again in heaven.

Check out these other similar titles...

A Pregnancy Devotional- I'm Praying for You: 40 Weeks of Scripture, Prayer and Reflection for Your Developing Baby- ISBN 978-0-692-05283-9

A Grandparent's Devotional- I'm Praying for You: 40 Weeks of Scripture, Prayer and Reflection for Your Developing Grandbaby- ISBN 978-1-7344708-5-7

Daughter, You are Treasured and Loved: 40 Weeks of Scripture, Prayer and Reflection for My Cherished Daughter- ISBN 978-1-7344708-3-3

Son, You are Esteemed and Loved: 40 Weeks of Scripture, Prayer and Reflection for My Incredible Son- ISBN 978-1-7344708-4-0

Each of the above books have similar prayer themes. In each book the scripture and prayer content is modified and tailored to the audience. Many of the writing prompts are different depending on the book. So, if you are thinking about which to buy, I would suggest choosing between a pregnancy devotional or a book for a child already born rather than to buy both for the same child. Keeping in mind that these books were created to foster opportunities for personalized input, you can definitely buy one for each child in your family or one for an unborn sibling and another for an already born child. Also, even though some (not all) of the prayers are similar, most of the prompts are very different between the unborn vs born books. Because of this, you may want to give another personalized book to the same child a few years down the road after the child is born.

For a child/teen in foster care or a child/young adult being mentored...

Praying You are Rooted and Growing: 25 Days of Biblical Truths with My Prayers and Notes of Encouragement for You- An Amazing Young Woman- ISBN 978-1-7344708-6-4

Purpose and Hope with God as Your Captain: 25 Days of Biblical Truths, with My Prayers and Notes of Encouragement for You- An Amazing Young Man- ISBN 978-1-7344708-7-1

Sharing the good news and gospel of Jesus Christ...

In Dark Uncertainty, Know the Light of the World: 13 Days of Biblical Truths of the Christian Faith, with My Prayers and Notes of Encouragement for You- ISBN 978-1-7344708-8-8